Deadly Triplets

A Theatre Mystery and Journal

ELI

EMERGENT LITERATURES

Deadly Triplets

A Theatre

Mystery and

Journal

Adrienne Kennedy

University of Minnesota Press · Minneapolis

Published by the University of Minnesota Press
2037 University Avenue Southeast, Minneapolis, MN 55414.
Printed in the United States of America.
Jacket and book design by Patricia M. Boman.

Library of Congress Cataloging-in-Publication Data

Kennedy, Adrienne.
  Deadly triplets : a theatre mystery and journal / Adrienne
Kennedy.
    p.   cm. — (Emergent literatures)
  ISBN 0-8166-1837-2
  I. Title. II. Series.
PS3561.E4252D4 1990
813'.54 — dc20   89-27996
                                                                CIP

The University of Minnesota is an
equal-opportunity educator and employer.

Contents

Preface

This book contains two very different, though connected, writings that deal with my experience of London and the theatre. Although a theatre journal and a theatre mystery may seem an unlikely combination, they are united in the attempt to write about a time and set of experiences that for me continue to be significant. The real mystery is perhaps why London has occupied such an important place in my imagination and why it continues to haunt me.

The "Theatre Journal," selections of which have been published as "London Sketches," was written long before the mystery began to take shape. Although I thought the sketches I had written on London were complete, four years later when I reread them I decided the sketches only reminded me of the mystery I still felt existed around London and my three-year stay there in 1966–1969. An avid fan of Sherlock Holmes, Agatha Christie, John Le Carré and, of course, Daphne Du Maurier (her novella *Don't Look Now* is one of my favorites), I decided to try a short mystery novel. Perhaps fiction in this form would finally capture the complexity of my feelings toward London.

I had notes on several mystery novels and stories and a play on Frankenstein. I read them over. Then I decided to use the London Sketches as a basis for a novel and call it *Deadly Triplets*.

Writing short sketches on people had seemed natural to me so I had been surprised when a friend (sometime during the four years) asked me why I had written sketches rather than a long continuous piece. I think I had written sketches because the people I met in the theatre seemed to be dream interludes in my life. My real continuous story seemed to be that of my family: my parents, my marriage, putting the children to bed, trying to read Beckett or Ionesco in the late hours, trying to write while my youngest son crawled on the floor with his toys.

The real me went out to Actor's Studio worrying about what to wear, running across the street to the cleaners, waiting for the babysitter, and met Geraldine Page, Rip Torn, Molly Kazan. These wonderful interludes of people excited me. But they were not quite real. Even with the passage of time most often the people I've met in the theatre seemed no more real to me than people I'd seen on stage at the old Palace Theatre in Cleveland when I was a kid.

There were other ways that writing more on London had continued to intrigue me. Over the years since 1969 I had often wondered why I had not wanted to write a screenplay about my life "in London as a Black woman," as the film producer had put it.

My plays were filled with the intricacies of race in my life. Why had I refused? Was it because at that moment I had not wanted race to separate me from the Brontës, Wordsworth . . . Tintern Abbey? (I often felt deep down that I had once lived in Haworth.) Yet race had permeated my work. In *Funnyhouse of a Negro,* my 1964 Obie-winning play, I had explored racial identity through my heroine Sarah. She had been torn enough about the question of race to kill herself. And Clara in *The Owl Answers* had been led to further madness by a summer trip to England (the home of her dead father's ancestors). My work was filled with English imagery — Queen Victoria, Chaucer, William the Conqueror — as it was filled with African images. Patrice Lumumba, savannahs, frangipani trees.

In Accra, Ghana, my husband and I had driven past the enclave of British homes surrounded by walls where British families had lived separate as they colonized the West African. Although in 1961 Nkrumah was Prime Minister, these enclaves still existed, and when we first arrived in Accra we even lived briefly in a section of the city that had once been populated by Europeans, a district of large homes, walled in, gardens tended by Ghanaians. I used this experience as the basis for plays and stories.

In thinking about starting a mystery novel I also remembered how defeated I felt the months before I left for London in 1966.

Theatre people and the famous had come out in the snow to see *Funnyhouse of a Negro,* but larger audiences stayed away. It closed after thirty-four performances. I had often thought my life was over. But right before the play closed the BBC had recorded it with Emlyn Williams narrating with the original off-Broadway cast. Diana Sands, who had lived in London while appearing in the West End, suggested that since *Funnyhouse* was recorded by the BBC I try to get an English production. She gave me more than a dozen names of very well-known theatre and movie producers and directors. She was interested in playing the lead role again as she had in the workshop production. My agent at William Morris said he would help. Diana was considered a great actress. After *Funnyhouse* closed, I had been supported by my husband even though we lived apart, but I soon received a Rockefeller Grant and commissions from Lincoln Center and Jerome Robbins. I had also applied for a Guggenheim; with this money I could go to England. I also had an idea for turning John Lennon's Nonsense Books into a play and had encouraging correspondence from his publisher. Although *Funnyhouse* was produced on the BBC I was not able to get a long-running production in London. However, William Gaskill produced the play in a weekend at the Royal Court, Jean Louis Barrault and his wife, Madeline Renaud, did put the play on in Paris at the Petit Odéon. And it was a major production.

I remembered many rapturous times in London, perhaps one of the happiest periods of my life. When I went back to Primrose Hill after a long while I wept at the sight of Chalcot Crescent, Regents Park Road, the zoo.

During my time there no one except a very old crazy woman in Rothwell Street had spoken to me negatively about race. And she in her half-consciousness had referred to me as Indian. Yet race was present in our consciousness. We talked about Vietnam, Malcolm X, Martin Luther King, the rally at the Roundhouse for jailed Wole Soyinka, went to the Ambiance and saw plays by Ed Bullins, discussed Michael X. At the same time I was treated grandly as a Guggenheim Fellow.

But I had lost the Lennon project (the adaptation of John Lennon's books, *In His Own Write* and *A Spaniard in the Works*), a project I initiated. I was told we would begin rehearsals in May. A friend called in March, "Why aren't you at the theatre?" she said. I explained rehearsals started in May. "They're rehearsing the play now," she said. I discovered there was nothing I could do. I had been dropped from the project but I was not protected; I was not a member of any British writers organization.

On the surface my life continued as a Guggenheim Fellow. I was commissioned to write a play for the Royal Court. I was invited everywhere. But now I felt I did not know the English. I remembered all of this. I remembered the wonderful teas at the Royal Court and I decided to make the Royal

Court Theatre at Sloane Square the major setting for my mystery novel: The Tower of London, the Thames, squares shrouded in mist, fog rising over Primrose Hill, stories of dead writers, dead Kings and Queens, landscapes with names like Gloucester Gate, Blenheim, Windsor, Madame Tussaud's, murders of Kings' wives, betrayals by archbishops and priests, Henry VIII, Sir Thomas More, Elizabeth and Essex, all of it still mesmerized me.

A Theatre Mystery
Deadly Triplets

Part One

I

Last night John Lennon was murdered at the Dakota apart-
ment in New York City four blocks from where I am now liv-
ing. I find it a strange and terrible coincidence that several
years ago I started writing a play based on Lennon's nonsense
books *In His Own Write* and *A Spaniard in the Works* in a
studio at the top of the Dakota apartments and that the writ-
ing of that play led to my being involved in a mysterious and
brutal death. A murder most unexpected.

My theatrical producers, who let me use the studio in the
Dakota to write, put me in touch with Lennon's English pub-
lisher. The publisher liked the pages of the play I had written.
This, and some reasons that I myself was not entirely aware
of, reasons that dealt with the strange demise of my adopted
mother years ago in England, convinced me that London was
the place I wanted to go. I brushed aside the unfulfilled long-
ing and curiosity that I had never satisfied about my adopted
mother's illness and last days and accepted my more obvious
reasons: I was recently divorced, in the throes of a new career
as an off-Broadway playwright, a career that was bringing me
recognition and the onslaught of theatre celebrities, and I had
just received a large writing grant. I gave up my apartment in
Greenwich Village, put my furniture in storage, and took my

two young sons to England. I wasn't to meet Lennon until many weeks later, but by that time I was entangled in the deadly ambitions and desires of other people I was yet to meet. I didn't know that my adopted sister, Antonia, whom I hadn't seen since I was eight years old, would seize my stay in London as the time when she would avenge the wrongs she thought I had done her. The time was spring 1967.

It was the time of British movies . . . *Ipcress File* . . . *Darling* . . . James Bond . . . *From Russia with Love* . . . *Goldfinger* . . . Jimi Hendrix . . . Carnaby Street, mini-skirts, Jean Shrimpton, Twiggy . . . British movie stars Michael Caine, Peter O'Toole, Albert Finney . . . the Rolling Stones and the Beatles. My boys had all the Beatles records and often we'd sit in their room and sing *I Wanna Hold Your Hand*.

As soon as I arrived in London I met with Lennon's publisher: I remember taking the underground from the Basil Street Hotel in Knightsbridge to Bedford Square. The offices were in a small house. The publisher and I talked in a dim, cluttered office, although outside the spring sun was bright.

"Miss Sand you have my permission to show your script of Lennon's books to theatrical producers," he said.

He was a middle-aged, dark-haired man in a black suit. Both he and his desk were almost gigantic enough to fill the small office. "If something comes of showing the script to theatrical producers then we can talk about terms." He shook my hand and out I went into the wonderful April afternoon, back to the Basil Street Hotel, a small, very charming hotel that seemed hidden away by Harrods.

My sons, seven and eight years old, were sitting in the tiny lobby talking to an elderly British gentleman in a military uniform who was attending an annual club banquet: The banquet had started in a lovely room beyond the lobby. The boys and I stood in the doorway and watched the men in uniform and the women in elegant formal dresses. The boys were delighted to see me. "Can we go to see a movie," they asked. We walked all the way to Leceister Square. We saw *Diamonds Are Forever.*

The next days I spent phoning agencies for a place to live. American Express had provided me with a list of places that were for rent. I also had called several people from the long list of theatre people I had compiled from American friends. I had lived in London, for three years, as a child but had forgotten almost everything about the city except an image of a long street with stone steps that led to a dark house . . . the house where I had lived with my adopted mother.

One of the people I called was a producer at a theatre in Hampstead that was always written about in *The Village Voice.* His name was Charlie Berman.

"Suzanne, I'd like to meet you. . . . I saw your play off-Broadway when I was in New York. . . . I loved it and would like to produce something of yours while you are in England. You know I produced Joe Orton's plays." Joe Orton was a writer who had been killed by his lover and people in the theatre still talked about it constantly. Berman and I agreed to meet the next Sunday.

"Suzanne, would you like to meet Joan Littlewood?" he asked before he hung up. "Also John Arden and his wife are friends of mine." And then he asked,

"Do you look at all like the picture of you that was in *Vogue* magazine last winter?"

"I think I do."

"You must be beautiful then."

"THANK YOU very much, Charlie."

I remembered the article in *Vogue,* in *People Are Talking About* . . . Suzanne Sand . . . playwright . . . twenty-eight, violet eyes, wavy masses of auburn hair, dark golden skin. She enchants those around her, something she seems unaware of. . . . One wonders is this the way Ethiopian princesses looked.

Her beauty amazes . . . and amazing too are her poetic gifts exhibited in her short play *The Heart of Alain Delon* presented off-Broadway and now in rehearsal at the Petit Odéon in Paris. She has a love of violet dresses . . . adores movies . . . and meeting famous people of which she keeps lists.

It was spring and I was abroad on a Guggenheim Grant. In the next days I found two floors of an exquisite house in Primrose Hill on a very pretty street . . . Chalcot Crescent. On the very day that I signed the lease I had an interview with the *Evening Standard*. The *Standard* did a short piece on me . . . American writer here on grant enchanted by England and Primrose Hill . . . they also mentioned my eyes which do look violet at times and the fact that I had lived in London briefly as a child when my adopted parents moved here from New York. It wasn't until a year later that I was to discover that this article in the *Standard* played a crucial part in shattering events that were to follow. And that I would regret that I had spoken about my life in the newspaper.

The article in the *Standard* also briefly summarized *The Heart of Alain Delon,* mentioning that it was to be presented soon in Paris at the Petit Odéon . . . the theatre headed by Jean Louis Barrault and his wife, Madeline Renaud.

The Heart of Alain Delon has as its heroine a young woman who possesses such intense dream waves that they reach the French actor by whom she is obsessed, on the set of *Purple Noon* where he is working. She remains by his side on the set of *Purple Noon,* a film about a young murdered American whose identity is taken.

Underlying these events are the powerful elements of mixed identity, desperation and death.

Victor Hamilton of the Royal Court is very interested in producing the play at the Court's soon-to-be-opened experimental theatre Upstairs at the Court.

II

Chalcot Crescent was beautiful. We lived on two floors of the house at No. 37. It was furnished and belonged to an English family who was in Nigeria. The faded parlor faced a wild garden with a brick wall. The boys had a large sunny room on the lower level. My room, the master bedroom, was the prettiest, shuttered and decorated in dark rose. All the houses on the curved crescent were painted white with regency fronts. Our door was a lovely yellow. My sons were thrilled because the television series *The Avengers* was filmed on the Crescent. The exterior of the corner house was used for the "Avengers" to emerge from and pursue their enemies. We all loved our house but we were afraid of the spiders in the bathrooms which were off the garden. We were happy.

The following week I met Alex Haley, visiting London to do research about his African ancestors, David Mercer, who wrote the screenplay for *Morgan,* and Kenneth Tynan who had written such brilliant reviews for *The New Yorker,* who now had a post at the National Theatre as dramaturg. I worked on my list of famous people.

And in June I wrote in my diary with the violet flowers on the cover:

I met James Eyre, star of The Aristocrat, *at a party in Little Venice given by the Bonhams, friends of my American producer. He invited me to lunch next Wednesday. I'm so excited and enchanted.*

James Eyre and I had lunch in a restaurant on Beauchamp Place: He invited me to come to the Royal Court Theatre and see him in a play called *Deadly Triplets*. Being with him filled me with delirium: while we were having lunch he went to make a phone call. Everyone in the restaurant stared at him. He was dazzling: tall, graceful, golden hair, extraordinary blue eyes. *The Aristocrat* had been one of the most admired movies of the last two years and had won a British Oscar.

"Now, Suzanne, I want to hear about everything you've been doing since you've been in London. Being a writer is something I really admire." I told him that I had been commissioned to write a play for Joseph Papp.

"And I hear you're working on a project of John Lennon's books."

"Yes."

"How marvelous. It must be wonderful to be a writer. The article about you in the *Evening Standard* said you lived here briefly as a child."

"I was adopted in the United States but my adoptive parents moved here. My adoptive mother died soon after we came here and I was sent back to the United States where I was raised by a wonderful man . . . a retired Army officer."

He stared into my face as I faltered.

"Well, I can sense you don't want to talk about it."

"It's just that my adopted mother died under very

strange circumstances and I am haunted by it. I dream of discovering how she died."

"And did she die here in London?"

"Yes. We lived in a large dark old house off Old Brompton Road."

"Have you been to see it?"

"Not yet."

"Then we must go there together. Perhaps we can even talk the present tenants into letting us inside so that you can see the rooms again." He smiled and leaned forward and took my hand.

We seemed to have so much in common. We both loved Fellini: we talked about the Italian director for the rest of our lunch, then he drove me back to Primrose Hill in his yellow Lotus. It promised to be a happy summer. I didn't know that on that very day someone I didn't know had made a trip to the house on Old Brompton Road . . . someone who wanted to know everything there was to know about me.

That afternoon Julia Lanier called. She was an American living in London after her divorce. She had started an off-Broadway theatre in New York and planned to produce some projects in London.

"I hear you're working on a project based on Lennon's books. Can you come to tea today, Adrian Gill, one of my best friends, who was in the Beatles movies is coming. He's a director and an actor. I thought perhaps the two of you should meet. Perhaps he can get Lennon interested in the project." The boys and I walked up to Hampstead in the green summer afternoon.

"Julie Lanier has sons too," I said. When we reached Hampstead they disappeared off into an enormous lush backyard.

Adrian Gill turned out to be a terribly funny man who did indeed know "John." He took the script I had written to John's house in Weybridge to ask Lennon's permission to show it to producers. Gill said we would all meet in a few weeks.

After the lunch on Beauchamp Place I didn't hear from James for several days although I did receive in the mail a record from him (the music from *La Strada*). Then one evening around six, just after the boys and I had come from a walk in Primrose Hill, he called.

"Suzanne, could you please come to the theatre tonight? I must talk to you."

III

The Royal Court Theatre looked majestic surrounded by the square of flowers. James was not backstage but was sitting on the red-carpeted stairs that led to the lounge where coffee and drinks were served during intermission of the plays.

"James, what is it?"

"Suzanne, come sit with me. Here I'll get you a coffee." He got up and brought me a small coffee from a silver pot that sat on a table.

"Did you get the music from *La Strada* that I sent you?" he smiled.

"Oh, yes I've played the music constantly. James is something wrong?"

At that moment someone wandered into the lounge and asked him for his autograph. After he left, James said, "There is something wrong. Can we go out after the theatre? I want to talk to you."

"Of course. I'll wait for you."

He headed for the doorway that led to the dressing rooms, turning just before he disappeared.

"You look so beautiful in that purple dress with your violet eyes and dark golden skin." And as he stood in the doorway he looked so slender, so blond, so perfect with his dazzling blue eyes, totally the image of the romantic Englishman.

"I'll go in and see the performance," I said.

The curtain went up on *Deadly Triplets*. The play had a chilling plot involving death and greed. The playwright, William Weldon, was one of the most admired young playwrights currently on the London scene: his plays were not quite as abstract as Edward Bond's or Pinter's but not as realistic as John Osborne's. He was very drawn to themes of mixed identity, ambition, and evil in contemporary life.

Deadly Triplets was two one-act plays under that title. The first was a curtain raiser, the second, *Deadly Triplets,* was the main play.

When I met Victor Hamilton, the head of the Royal Court, he remarked about the affinity between Weldon's work and my own. We used real people as a take-off for our plays and being killed for one's identity was a common theme. In Esslin's book *Theatre of the Absurd,* he gave a page to Weldon. Both these plays were cinematic, with powerful images and many things happening at once.

The second play, which took place in a modern version of an Elizabethan castle, went fine. But James did appear agitated and seemed to falter once, as if he were about to fall. For a moment it seemed that the side of his head was bleeding but then I realized that it was stage blood that he had accidentally smeared with his hands onto his temples. After the performance we went to the Daisy, a restaurant on the King's Road in Chelsea that was very popular.

"Suzanne, sometimes I believe I may be in danger."

"What sort of danger?"

"A danger that I can't define. Tonight I was so nervous that I got the blood from my hands all over my face. Sometimes I wonder is it working with Sarah?"

"Sarah?"

"She plays the queen . . . Sarah Constable Maxwell . . . we were once engaged and after it was over she wrote me some very anguished and dark letters. Sometimes I can see her watching me from the wings."

"Do you think she would harm you?"

"I don't know. But I was surprised to find she knows a great deal about you."

"About me?"

"Yes. She knows that your adopted mother was a woman called Gina Shirer, your adopted father a producer. She seems to know a great deal about them and even knows the person who lives in the house on Old Brompton Road.

"We were standing backstage when all of a sudden she started to talk about you."

I was afraid the article in the *Standard* had raised questions about me. It made me uneasy.

James sensed my fear. He took my hand. We ordered more drinks. The restaurant was pretty, the table round and covered with pale-blue linen cloth. In a mood that was to persist when I was with James, people and events became hazy almost as if I were hypnotized. I was half aware that the movie actor Richard Harris sat at a nearby table with a girl in a white dress. Twiggy came in. Some people were dancing and Mia Farrow came up and spoke to James for a second, then we were alone again.

"James, will you still go to the house on Old Brompton Road with me?"

"Of course I will. We'll go soon. It seems a theatre photographer lives there now. In fact, I think I've met him once or twice. His name is John Sharples."

We talked no more that night of the danger he sensed. But in the intoxicating golden light of the restaurant I couldn't stop staring at the slight trace of stage blood still on the edge of his blond hairline.

Suddenly he said, "Do you know that woman over there?" I turned. "There's a woman seated against the wall by the door. She's been watching us." I turned. But she was gone.

Sitting in Primrose Hill while the boys fly kites, I work on my list:

Tea at playwright John Arden's

We sat in an upstairs parlor . . . a lovely Sunday. The boys and the Ardens' beautiful children run up and down the stairs.

James told me that he heard Weldon is writing a new play. And that Weldon is very secretive about the nature of the play. It will be called *Deadly Triplets Again*. And it does have a role which both Weldon and Victor Hamilton are hoping James will consider. James says he believes Weldon has shown Hamilton parts of the new play, but, of course, Hamilton is quite secretive too. They are hoping the play will be the big attraction at the Court next year and have already approached one or two other well-known actors. It seems there is again a role for Marianne Faithfull, whom Hamilton used in *The Three Sisters*.

James says he's positive Weldon is showing Hamilton pages of a rough draft as he finishes them and that he heard the play will further explore historical characters as symbols and create a plot from fact and Weldon's own imagination just as he had done in *Deadly Triplets*.

There were rumors that Hamilton spoke to Laurence Harvey about a role. Hamilton loved putting "film stars" in his plays and had been searching for a play that might possibly star Marianne Faithfull and Mick Jagger.

IV

For a while there was no talk of danger: living in Primrose Hill was a joy. James came in the late afternoons when he had finished talking about doing a new movie in Chelsea.

"We must go to Rome one day and meet Fellini," he said.

He gave me a book of Fellini's screenplays in Italian. And we listened again and again to the music of Nino Rota, sitting in my parlor that overlooked the wild garden. We walked in Regent's Park, in Hyde Park, in Kensington Gardens, we went to the Orangerie.

"You're a writer," James often said. "Maybe that's why I find it so easy to talk to you." I discovered his father was a novelist and a lawyer and lived on Eaton Terrace. His parents were divorced. His mother lived somewhere on the edge of London in a house "far too large for someone living alone, with a tennis court that is overgrown with weeds. I've told them about you. And they want to meet you." He also had an older brother named Michael who lived in New York. Both of them had gone to the Royal Academy of Dramatic Arts.

"He's a far better actor than I am," James said. "He went to America in the company of *Look Back in Anger* and decided to stay there."

As he promised, James called about visiting South Kensington.

"I think it's time we went out to Old Brompton Road," he said.

The house on Old Brompton Road was reached by a flight of stone steps. John Sharples let us in.

"Oh, James Eyre," he said. "I'm quite a fan of yours." Inside the dark hallway were photographs of cats. Sharples was an amiable, heavy-set man, balding and effeminate.

"Miss Sand would you like to see your old room?" We went up the long flight of stairs to the dark rooms on the third floor: my old room with the emerald-green marble fireplace faced a garden that could only be entered with a key. I remembered all the rooms on this floor were dark. The room was almost empty except for some sketches that Sharples said he was planning to frame. I remembered the smell of the gas that had lit the fireplace. I wanted to see the room where I had last seen my adopted mother, Gina, pale, dark circles under her eyes, lying with her head on a white pillow.

"I'm going to the hospital, Suzanne. Be a good girl." I never saw her again.

"That room is my studio now." Sharples led us down to the second floor. Gina's old room was a clutter of chairs, prints, photographs, and camera equipment. In the corner was a photographer's umbrella. My stepparents had often fought in this room of chaise lounges and Gina's prints of Renoir ... Gina sitting on her bed, or pacing the floor. Sharples hurried us out. "I do have a rather important appointment," he said.

"There is one thing," he led us back down the stairs and through the kitchen into a backyard that was rampant with stone statues and fountains broken in disrepair.

"I must do something about this garden," he muttered as he opened a large wooden door in the ground that led to the cellar.

"There is a trunk here." Inside the damp bin was a dark brown, flat trunk covered in moss. James let himself into the bin and after a time pried the trunk open. The inside, lined with the rotting remains of lavender wallpaper, was empty except for a few summer shawls, a child's white organdy dress, and a wooden cane. We had almost closed it when I picked up the child's dress wondering had it been mine. A tiny gold frame fell to the ground. James picked it up. There was a photograph of a young, dark-haired woman.

"Do you know who this is?" he asked.

"Yes, that's Antonia . . . my adopted sister."

"Where have I seen her?"

"She used to be a famous fashion model. I think she's retired now. She was eight years older than me . . . she was the Shirer's only child and I fear was made greatly unhappy by their adopting me."

James stared at the picture of Antonia. We closed the bin.

On the drive back to Regents Park we talked.

"I'm afraid coming here has been very disturbing to you," James said. "Suzanne, perhaps we shouldn't come again. It's not wise to look back too much." He took my hand as we drove. And asked what had happened after my adopted mother's death.

"Shirer didn't want me so I was sent to New York and adopted again by Captain Sand. We lived in Long Island."

"And your real parents?"

"I know nothing of them. Gina and Shirer got me from an agency that had a great many children of mixed birth."

That afternoon was the only time we ever made love.

The children and I went to the movies. *West Side Story* was at the Marble Arch. They loved *McKenna's Gold*. We went often to the zoo . . . we loved the leopards. We went to Madame Tussaud's. At home we'd watch *The Saint* on TV. James phoned me nightly after the performance. He talked about how many people were in the theatre or "my concentration wasn't its best tonight" or "my work in the play isn't what I hoped it would be." And then one night he said, "Tonight of all nights, my brother Michael showed up at the theatre. I didn't even know he was in London until I saw him sitting in the last row staring at me with that critical eye of his. He didn't even wait to say hello afterwards but just went off. That's so like him."

Everything would have seemed to be all right except that James had fallen on the stage a number of times. One night he fell against a huge metal chest and got a long gash above his left eye.

Adrian Gill and I met again with the director of the theatre. I gave him the new pages of the play. He said he liked them very much and by December we would have a Sunday performance, then we could see if the script worked. I promised I would have the final pages in three weeks. Soon after Gill phoned to say the head of the theatre did indeed like my pages but he also thought it would be nice if Lennon worked on the script.

"What does that mean?"

"I don't know. We'll have to wait and see." He hung up.

Often James was melancholy and mistrustful. He said he thought very often the staff of the theatre was patronizing to him. And perhaps it hadn't been such a good idea after all to accept this role, but that Hamilton loved him so in *The Aristocrat* that he had convinced him he could do it. It saddened me to hear him say this because the staff of the theatre actually doted on James.

"James, they adore you." A fury came into his blue eyes.

"Perhaps they do adore me but they don't really respect my work. I don't really have enough stage experience." I asked him how his new film was going.

"It's chaos. They've changed producers again."

Sometimes he'd say, "You know, Suzanne, you've become my dearest friend."

Often my former husband would call from New York or Washington. He was an officer with a government agency.

"You sound strange, Suzanne. Is something wrong?"

I got a note from John Sharples. And in the note was enclosed a photograph of the house on Old Brompton Road. I have to go to Amsterdam, the note said, but I've become very interested in your emotional quest to uncover the sad details of your mother's death. There may be some other photographs that exist. I will call you when I return from Amsterdam. I want to help you.

I know you will find some of the answers you seek in this old photograph that I found in the lining of the wallpaper of the trunk. Can that child be you, clinging to the woman who I'm sure must be Gina?

The faded photograph appeared to be the house in the 1940s. I remembered the hedge was short and those were the shutters on the windows that had been slightly shattered by the bombing of London during the war.

And the happiest part: Gina stood in the doorway, in a coat with a fur collar. And standing beside her was a child.

Although I had no pictures of myself until I had gone to live with Captain Sand, I believed it to be me. I started to cry. I had never seen a picture of my mother and myself. I could hardly wait to tell James.

The trip to Old Brompton Road never left my mind. Yet I didn't sense that Sharples was as important as he would prove to be.

V

When I didn't hear from Sharples in a week, I felt I had to find him. I wanted to go to Holland.

I arrived in Amsterdam just as it was turning dark, too late to really search out the theatres for Sharples. In the morning, I thought, I will set out and go to every theatre in the city.

My pension was on the canal near the Leidseplein. And at the Leidseplein there was a theatre showing a modern production of *Frankenstein*. Before dinner I stood for a long time studying the posters outside the theatre trying to find Sharples's name. I knew a production of *Frankenstein* might have complex visuals and photo montages. His name was nowhere. But after I had dinner at the American Hotel I decided to go and see the production anyway.

I arrived just as the curtain went up. The theatre was disorienting and spare with sharp horizontal benches for seats.

The curtain opened on a dim drawing room as Mary Shelley sat weaving a wreath of dried flowers. Then another Mary Shelley character entered. It appeared that she was Mary Shelley's twin sister who had just arrived from France.

The play was a modern version of Mary Shelley and Fran Kenstein, written by an experimental Dutch playwright named Huis, the stage was covered in a black cloth and the set designer had used contemporary white furniture. Film excerpts from the old classic versions of *Frankenstein* were used flashing at the center of the stage. The deaths and the staging of the deaths were particularly brutal and spotlighted in harsh stagelight that flickered off and on to convey a sense of dream images. In the Huis play Mary Shelley had a twin who posed as Mary Shelley in order to murder and ravage her enemies, wooing them with sweet letters of poetry. The play was an imaginative conundrum and exceptionally violent.

That night I lay awake in the room facing the canal, remembering the crying, the weaving of dried flowers, the dual plot concerning Elizabeth and Victor in the actual story of *Frankenstein*. I could not sleep.

James had said that along with a sense of danger he had dreamed over and over that someone near him had a double or twin identity. Yet he knew no twins except Sarah Constable Maxwell and her sister Ingrid.

The next morning James called from London. He said he was worried about me, but called to say that he had gotten the names of the theatres in Amsterdam that Sharples often worked for, photographing productions and doing still photography. But one theatre in particular was the most important, an avant-garde theatre near the Prinsengracht. James had actually seen a production there several months ago, for which, he remembered now, Sharples had done a massive group of arresting visuals. It was a production that had quite an underground following in Amsterdam. The play, he said, was a series of bird monologues performed by a woman who called herself "Anna Karenina." It contained a collection of brilliant drawings and photographs created to depict the lives of birds of prey. It had been running in Amsterdam several months near the Prinsengracht, around the corner from the Anne Frank House. The actress did eerie lyric monologues of birds, recalling their lives and their haunts. And he was sure that was where I would find Sharples. I decided to stay in Amsterdam one more night.

"Suzanne, I apologize for not remembering this earlier," he said. "I believe the name of the theatre is the Miko."

After a breakfast of cold meats and chocolate I set out walking. And as I walked through Amsterdam the images of violence and vengefulness that had permeated the *Frankenstein* play obsessed me. I went to the Rijksmuseum and saw the Vermeers. In the afternoon I went to the Anne Frank House but all the time thinking about Sharples. Why was I so determined to find him? I didn't know. Why did I want to confront him? He had been nothing but polite and helpful. I really didn't understand why I had followed him to Amsterdam. As I walked inside the Anne Frank House, climbing the steep stairs behind the cupboard door which led to the hidden annex, I thought of Sharples. As I stood in the room of World War II photographs and scenes of war, starvation, and man's anger and cruelty, I thought of Sharples. Why? I asked myself.

After dinner at the American Hotel I set out for the Miko Theatre. The owner of my pension had made a map for me. It was cold: the shadows of the canal, the trolley cars, the darkness filled me with suspense and expectancy. If Sharples was the photographer for this play, perhaps he came to the theatre every night. He appeared to be a gregarious man, a man who might well enjoy being at the performance each night, going out with the actors after the theatre closed.

Finally, just as James had said, on a street near the Prinsengracht was an iron door, almost hidden, except for two black and white posters attached to it.

MIKO

Birds of Prey

with

"Anna Karenina"

and in smaller letters but distinctly

Visual effects
by John Sharples
Box office opens at 7:00
Performance begins at 8:00

It was only 6:45. So I waited until 7:00, when a young girl with long hair and a heavy coat opened the iron door.

The theatre was an open space painted white. Several people started to gather, all sitting on the floor. In the center of the space was a giant cubicle from which the actress was soon to emerge. Again I had the feeling that this evening too had a direct relationship to my life. I seated myself on the floor waiting for the performance to begin and just as the lights went down I saw Sharples. He entered the theatre from behind the cubicle and came walking along the side of the now darkened space, obviously coming from backstage, and sat in a chair at the edge of the theatre almost parallel to the cubicle.

The performance piece was a dazzling series of narratives on *Birds of Prey*. The actress's entire body, including her face, was transformed into a bird; the costume and mask were of extremely delicate and beautiful colors and interpretations of the birds were spell-binding yet frightening. That was their appeal.

She sang a description of herself:

> Arctic owls, whose courtship takes
> place by the light of the midnight sun
> often give aerial displays.
>
> Small birds of prey position
> themselves above and behind a larger
> one, crossing their territory. By
> means of darting and screaming they
> try to move the intruder on.

It seemed when she said "intruder" she looked into my eyes. I felt a strong connection between myself and this savage experimental piece.

As she went on, I thought what kind of actress would create such a piece? For although it was brilliant, it was filled with ugliness.

"Anna Karenina" changed costumes rapidly. Now she appeared as an elf owl singing.

She sang as a forest bird under attack. She was a thrilling performer: her timing, her execution of movement perfect. I admired her. She possessed the ability to convey mystery and fear, attacking and assaulting the audience. There was a fierceness and sadness in her work that I understood.

During the short intermission, I remained seated but I could still see Sharples.

Just before the lights had come on he had disappeared behind a curtain at the rear of the space but now had returned to his chair parallel to the cubicle. Somehow I lost sight of him as the play started. Again during the second half of the evening the bird narratives seemed about to illuminate a secret within myself. For a moment I thought perhaps this was Gina. But that was ridiculous. "Anna Karenina" was a young woman.

Although her face and body were covered, I was convinced she was in her twenties.

The performance ended abruptly. She walked to the rear curtain and disappeared, but not before I saw she and Sharples embrace. The audience was surprised and waited for her to take a curtain call. Suddenly a young man came through the space and stood by the cubicle.

"Anna Karenina isn't felling well," he said. "She thanks you but will be unable to take her curtain call. Goodnight."

All the lights came up. People in the audience, still surprised, slowly got to their feet and started to exit the theatre. I stood for an instant gazing at the rear curtain, but I knew Sharples was gone. They both were gone.

I returned to London that night feeling very disappointed.

VI

The next evening I sat in the dressing room at the Court waiting for James to come off stage. He entered behind me; I watched him in the mirror of the dressing table. It was always strange to see him with the dark wig he wore in the play. He also wore plain black modern pants and shirt that was the costume for *Triplets*. He looked tired. It was an exhausting role, in which he played three roles . . . the triplets who return to haunt and destroy their murderer. Often he said, "I'm exhausted." He sat down beside me where I was working on pages of the play I was writing for the Public Theatre.

"Suzanne, a lot is happening that I don't understand." He lowered his head and covered his face with his hands: the dark hair and heavy make-up made him look like the villain he had played on stage a few moments before. I begged him to please talk to me, to tell me what was troubling him. But at that moment he had to go back on stage. When he returned he acted as if he had never spoken.

"Friends of my family are in the audience," he said vaguely.

Suddenly he said, "This Antonia, it's been bothering me where I've seen her. I think she's a friend of Vicki's. I'm sure of it. You know Vicki was a model in New York also and I'm positive Antonia is a friend of hers. It seems to me that Vicki has a picture of them all at a party in New York. It used to be on her dresser. I looked for it but I didn't see it."

I knew that James's wife, Vicki, was a former model from New York and was eleven years older than he. (James was thirty.) She had formerly been married to a movie producer who had deserted her and left her with two young children.

"She dotes on James," Sarah Constable Maxwell had said to me backstage one evening.

I was disturbed that James's wife Vicki might know Antonia Shirer. For in all my life I had never met anyone who had hated me the way Antonia had. And I had violent, troubled dreams of her.

"I'm going to find that picture," he said. "It's disappeared."

I hadn't seen Antonia since the day after Gina had died.

"You killed my mother, " she said. "It's because of you my parents quarreled. You killed her."

After Gina's death Antonia had gone off to Chelsea to live with her father. Gina and Shirer had been separated, and I always felt the reason Gina had adopted me had been because she was so estranged from both Shirer and her daughter Antonia. And the reason she had loved me so much.

We sat in the dressing room and talked while James removed the stage make-up.

"John Sharples sent me a photograph. And, James, it's my mother and me," I said, not knowing the savage, cruel connection there was between the photograph that James couldn't find and the photograph I held in my hand. I held up the photo under the dressing-table lights. James seem puzzled.

"What's wrong?" I asked. He studied the photograph as he dried his face.

"Can I keep this for a day or so?" he asked.

I was so preoccupied that I had practically stopped seeing people except possibly Ann. She was an American and ran a theatre in Rome with some friends and was working on an Italian translation of a play of mine.

"Suzanne, you're looking awfully tense. Why don't you come out with us sometime. Robert and I are having dinner with some wonderful Kuwaitis he works with." Her husband, Robert, worked with an oil company. She disappeared back to her house in Ennismore Gardens until the next time she came to show me the translation. I yearned to confide in her but I didn't. If only I had.

"You're even more distracted this week." She asked had I gotten in with a crowd that took LSD. I said, no, I took no drugs but I probably was drinking a little too much. She convinced me to go to the ballet with them. We saw Nureyev.

Wrote in my diary: Filmways, a movie company, called. Have an interview. They're interested in doing a movie about Americans in London.

At that time I began to get odd phone calls, a silence and then the person would hang up. I did tell Ann about them.

"Perhaps they're from Victoria Eyre," she said. Ann had met James leaving my house one afternoon. " I've heard she's uncontrollably jealous of him."

The secretary from the theatre called. John Lennon hadn't left for India yet. There was to be a meeting between the artistic director of the theatre, Gill, Lennon, and myself. I took the Underground to the theatre.

We sat cramped in straight chairs at the artistic director's desk. Lennon repeated that the idea of the play appealed to him because of the lasting life of a play. It was settled that the project would be continued while he was in India. Lennon's chauffeur dropped him off in Belgravia then drove Gill and myself to Primrose Hill.

It would be a year before I discovered why James was puzzled when he saw the photograph John Sharples had sent me of my mother and myself.

The Petit Odéon wanted me to come to Paris for the opening of *The Heart of Alain Delon*. I looked forward to meeting Jean Louis Barrault and his wife, Madeline Renaud. I went to Harrods to buy a violet fall coat I had seen and even had my hair cut at Sassoons.

VII

James finally found the picture of Antonia.

"It was on the piano. I don't know why. Except Vicki often practices her Chopin Etudes in the evening when I'm at the theatre."

It was a photograph of people at a formal party, people sitting on a couch posing in evening clothes. It appeared to be about ten years old . . . the time when both Antonia and Vicki Eyre had filled the fashion pages. I had not seen Antonia since that last day on Old Brompton Road, but I often had had dreams of her. Yet I still saved the *Vogue* magazines she appeared in . . . I had followed in the gossip columns her first marriage to a photographer and her long affair with a movie star . . . but in recent years had lost track of her. It seemed she lived either in Italy or in Los Angeles. Throughout the years I had always felt I would see her again. I dreamed of Antonia one night. In the morning when I awakened James called. . . . He was calling from his father's house on Eaton Terrace. He had collapsed on stage the night before and would miss his performances for a while until he discovered what was wrong with him. His brother Michael who was still in London would be playing James's role in *Deadly Triplets*.

James assured me he would call as soon as he saw the doctor. He did call later . . . the doctor could find nothing wrong with him, but James's father insisted that he totally rest for a few days.

"By the way, I did mention Antonia Shirer to Vicki. She is living in Italy now. I will try to get her address. Perhaps you could write to her and meet and reconcile. I think that would make you happy." Before we finished talking I told James I wanted to go and see his brother on stage.

"He'll be pleased."

I had a desire to see Michael Eyre. Perhaps I could talk to him. I sensed by now that James was hiding something and that I could not help him unless I knew more.

Before I left for the theatre James called again. I went down into the rose bedroom and took the call.

"Did Gina die the day you saw her?"

"No, in fact she went to the hospital and came home again but I was not allowed to see her. She was kept in the drawing room on a day bed by the window and cared for by an Irish nurse. I know because the bed remained there after she died."

"And Shirer visited her?"

"He came daily. And always I could hear him say to the nurse, 'Let no one into this room.' "

"And you never entered the drawing room the entire time."

"No."

"How long do you think she was there before she died?"

"I'm not sure but often I could hear her calling me. 'Suzanne, Suzanne.' I would run down the stairs and stand outside the drawing room door but the nurse would appear. And I was sent upstairs."

"Then suddenly one morning I came downstairs, the drawing room doors were open. I was overjoyed, running across the room, thinking I saw her. But she was gone. And there was blood on the floor."

"Shirer never explained anything to you."

"I never saw him after that. His secretary came. She explained that Gina had died and that soon I would be going back to the United States."

"You were in the house a few days after Gina's death."

"Perhaps a week or so."

"Did anything else happen?"

"No, except sometimes I'm positive I heard someone laughing."

"Laughing? And just you and the nurse were in the house?"

"Yes. But I know it, James, there was laughter that came from the old bedroom, the one that John Sharples has turned into a studio."

"Whose laughter?"

"It was Gina's, James, I'm sure it was."

"Gina's?"

"Did you go to the funeral?"

"No. . . . All I remember is one day the nurse came in a black coat. 'Poor Mrs. Shirer,' she said, 'poor Mrs. Shirer.' "

James was silent.

"Perhaps she's still alive," he said.

"But that's impossible."

"Maybe not. Go and enjoy the theatre. We'll talk tonight."

Of course I was in an agitated mood after what James had said about Gina. And I still wondered if James's doctor was right about his health. As I watched Michael on stage that night, I thought of James and his intense love and involvement in *Deadly Triplets*, his hard work on the role and his concern that he portray the triplets accurately. "It's based on history, you know. I can't seem to bring the power it needs.

Someone like Paul Scofield could do it justice." James was very sensitive about not having finished the Royal Academy of Dramatic Art before he started getting offered small roles in movies. Unlike Michael he had dropped out of school to play a role in *Darling,* one in *Dr. Zhivago* and then *The Aristocrat.* That night the power of *Triplets* was overwhelming . . . the greed . . . the ambition of the characters was brilliantly portrayed through Michael Eyre's performance.

Sitting near me was the playwright, Bill Weldon, watching Michael as he played the second triplet, the one who returns to drive the King's young, beloved wife insane as he takes revenge. The dead triplets are in the mind of the King, but they become apparitions so powerful that he accidentally causes his only son to jump from a cliff, and drives his wife to madness and finally kills himself. They had been his three dear nephews, and he had them murdered so he could obtain the crown of England. The most exciting aspect of *Triplets* was watching one actor play each of the triplets as he returned from the grave. Weldon watched Michael intently.

I admired Weldon's work very much: I had met him at a tea given for him by the Royal Court soon after I met James; he was a polite, quiet man with piercing brown eyes. He lived in a cottage in Yorkshire, and when I had visited Haworth, the home of the Brontës, I had visited his nearby house. How strange the small, remote cottage had been, with its dim interior, small windows, and dark battered furniture. Even though it had been summer, the cottage inside was very cold. Weldon and I drank gin and tonics and he told me stories of the surrounding area. "You'll want to visit Beatrix Potter's home next time," he said. "It's very near here, though I suspect Haworth and the Brontës will always be what most people want to see."

"I'm glad we're getting this chance to really talk," he said. "You know our writing in many ways is similar. We are both obsessed with lost identity and uncontrollable hatred." In the twilight he took me for a wonderful walk on the moors surrounding his cottage.

During intermission, much to my surprise, there was a note from Michael Eyre brought to me by one of the ushers. It said that he had recognized me, from the stage, from a photograph in *The New York Times* and could I meet him backstage after the play. There was something urgent he wanted to talk to me about.

In the lobby Victor Hamilton, the head of the Court, rushed up to me.

"Wasn't Michael Eyre superb? James is a fine, romantic actor but Michael has a kind of madness about him."

"Yes, he was very good."

"He's a wonderful actor. I don't know why he's stayed in America. We all want him to come back to England." Hamilton reminded me that there would be a tea Thursday at the Court for John Osborne and he hoped I would come.

"There will be a lot of Americans there, Ellen Stewart, Sam Shepard, Joe Chaikin. You know all of them, don't you?"

"Yes."

"You Americans are taking over London. And, oh, Suzanne, tonight I'm having a small party . . . one of the Beatles, George Harrison, and his wife, Patti, have promised to come. My house is near Baker Street. Here's the address."

Michael emerged from James's dressing room just as I came backstage. He put out his hand to me and smiled.

"I'm happy to meet you. You know I'm quite an admirer of your work. In fact, I saw a workshop of *The Heart of Alain Delon* three years ago when it was done at the Actors Studio. I was an observer there for a season." He said he had also seen the play when it was off-Broadway and was fascinated by the difference in the productions. He was shorter than

James, a few years older, darker hair, yet still very handsome. The resemblance was remarkable.

"And the complexity with which the play dealt with identity." He continued talking, suddenly suggesting we have a drink together.

We went to the pub next door to the Court and ordered vodka tonics.

"I'm very worried about my brother," he said. "As a matter of fact, we are all very troubled and that's why I wanted to talk to you. I know you see him a great deal and I thought maybe you just might be able to shed a little light on his state of mind. We fear he's having some sort of breakdown. You know last night after he collapsed on stage and was taken home, he actually accused his wife, Vicki, of trying to kill him, saying he had collapsed because she has been poisoning him and that's why he's been fainting. He went on ranting about how he's kept it to himself but he's not going to any longer and on and on. You know James is the youngest and we all adore and worship him and are proud of his big success. We all know that Vicki is very jealous of him and has periods of the bleakest depression because she often feels he doesn't care about her . . . but to attack her in that kind of outburst is unforgivable."

He asked me had I observed anything strange about James's behavior.

"I only know that he has been despondent at times and certainly I've been aware of his falling on stage."

"But he hasn't accused anyone of trying to kill him?"

"No."

"We're worried because we also know that he's trying desperately to follow up his success in *The Aristocrat*. You know there are just the two of us and we've always shared each other's problems. I'm just so worried."

"I will do anything I can to help," I said. He smiled.

"Thank you, Suzanne."

"Anything at all."

He asked me how I liked London. And we discussed New York. Michael knew a great deal about Black culture. We talked about Miles Davis, Paul Robeson. He especially liked Eric Dolphy. He said that after living in New York two years he had begun to miss London. We ordered more drinks and he asked me would I like to go out to dinner.

"I'm going to a party at Victor Hamilton's. Perhaps another time."

"By the way," he said, "you know Vicki adores writers and she's heard so much about you. She'd love to meet you. Americans are still her closest friends although she's been over here a long time. And she sees herself as somewhat of a writer." I said I would like to meet her.

"One thing, Suzanne, James must not know about this meeting. This must be secret between us, this meeting we've had. It's better for James." He smiled. His eyes were dark, not blue, as James's were. The pub had filled up with people from the Royal Court.

"I'd heard how beautiful you were and you are, and what a lovely violet dress." He smiled again. And at that moment I realized that I had seen him somewhere before tonight. We said good-bye. And I took a taxi to Baker Street.

The next afternoon there was a piece in the *Evening Standard* that said they lamented that Michael Eyre, who was so brilliant in the roles of the Triplets in William Weldon's play *Deadly Triplets* at the Royal Court, had gone to America to live and they thought he should return to the London stage. Eyre, who is replacing his brother James, it went on to say, has the subtlety and mystery of a young Alec Guinness.

I wanted to talk to Michael again. I realized I hadn't even gotten his address. I wanted to know more about James. A few nights later I went back to Sloane Square determined to find him, but Michael was gone. The stage manager said that Michael suddenly had to leave for New York and an understudy would be playing James's role a few more nights until he returned.

Then late that night Michael called from Heathrow airport.

"Suzanne," he said "something terrible happened . . . I believe James may be trying to harm Vicki . . . in fact, I believe he may be trying to kill her. I will write you. I must get my plane."

The next morning Sharples called back from Amsterdam.

"I think I have proof," he said, "that your mother did not die when you think she did. I have to go to California. I will call you when I come back."

Before I could question him he was gone.

I realized now I had chosen to come to England to solve the heart-breaking mystery of Gina's death. Gina, who in spite of her brief time in my life, was the only mother I'd known. I was so happy I had James to help me.

VIII

Yet increasingly I couldn't sleep. My nights were disturbed with restless thoughts.

Sometimes I saw "Anna Karenina" running around the cubicle, heard her odd soprano voice cry out:

> *Among the hawkling birds the male*
> *and the female are almost the same*
> *size. But among most raptors the*
> *females are larger than the males.*
> *The way of hunting and killing is still*
> *the same for both sexes.*

I dreamed of the Mary Shelley twins in the Frankenstein play on the Leidseplein and always the Anne Frank House and the canals of Amsterdam. I saw myself sitting in Anne Frank's room with her movie-star pictures on the wall. Then I would descend the stairs to the warehouse and hit my head against the cupboard door. One time "Anna Karenina" and I were having tea at the table in the Frank's kitchen. Suddenly "Anna

Karenina" started to run around the table screaming, "Help us escape, Suzanne."

I took out the map that the owner of the pension had given me. It said:

Singel

Heerengracht

Keizersgracht

Prinsengracht

When I awoke I would try to work on my list of famous people.

Laurence Olivier wore a brown suit with a vest. When he spoke to me he took my hand.

Ringo Starr was a small man with piercing eyes.

Viscount Julius said when he was a child "Winston" came to visit his parents.

Marsha Hunt, the model in Vogue *(when I commented on how beautiful she was) said she understood perfectly the illusion of applying make-up.*

I saw Sean Connery at a play at the National Theatre.

I saw Michael Caine at Christie's. They were auctioning Diaghilev's drawings.

In the middle of one of these nights James phoned. He had remembered something about Antonia.

"I didn't realize until today," he said, "that a boy and girl who once came to the house in Little Venice were Antonia's children. They were both dark-haired and silent.

"I remember both wore rings with curved insignias. It was a few years ago, when I first met Vicki. When she introduced us, Vicki said their mother was an old friend of hers who lived in America and that she was in London on business and the children were visiting for the day. They were very silent children with the darkest hair and a pallor in their skin. Vicki said they had once lived nearby on Maida Avenue. They had this collection of rings that they were playing a game with; rings with the curved insignias. And one of them . . . the boy had a falcon on his shoulder. It was startling. But he made no mention of it. They just sat on a bench in the middle of the drawing room.

"Later when I mentioned the children, I remember Vicki said they lived somewhere in the country with their father . . . the Viscount Manasséi.

"As far as I know their father is Viscount Manasséi. It seems he was the first man Antonia was ever really involved with and these children are his. He and Antonia never married. She was very young and the Viscount was married when these children were born. It was before she left England to go to America. I don't remember their names. All I remember is that Vicki said one child was dedicated to Antonia and the other child loathed the mother and despised being the illegitimate child of a Viscount. When I made a remark about their strangeness, she said, perhaps it's because they don't know their mother. She comes only once or twice a year to see them. Their father and his wife adopted them and they all live quite isolated in the country. Perhaps that's why they are so silent

. . . the girl with her rings . . . the boy with his falcon. Perhaps that's why."

IX

James promised me that he would find out exactly where Antonia's children lived. He said he realized that he had often seen their father, the Viscount Manasséi, at dinner parties in London but they had never spoken. The Viscount was a journalist and an expert on Turkish painting.

Late at night I awakened more and more. I kept the frayed theatre program from *Birds of Prey* in a Victorian letter box I bought on Portobello Road, and when I couldn't sleep I would read and reread the text of the biography of "Anna Karenina."

Program

"Anna Karenina" lives somewhere in London in the Islington section. She prefers to keep her real name a bit of a mystery . . . choosing to let her birds express her identity. She will say, though, that she loves the theatre and performing and feels she was born to be an actress, something she only realized in her early twenties, the time before that she considers a loss. At a fortunate moment

several years ago she met two people who
influenced and totally changed her life.

Her birds of prey, she says, are real to her like a
family . . . she feels she has a relationship with her
"family of birds" and the birds of prey have a
relationship with one another . . . often violent
relationships.

Then lightly, at the end of the program, "Anna Karenina"
was quoted as saying:

"If I did not have my birds I might murder."

Before the end of the paragraph there was a middle pas-
sage that talked about how when "Anna Karenina" worked in
Amsterdam she visited the Anne Frank House daily because
Anne Frank was an inspiration to her, Anne Frank's writing
and Anne's ability to transcend adversity.

On the back of the program was a note from the pro-
ducer of *Birds of Prey* . . . a Mr. Coigney. It said:

"Anna Karenina's" Birds of Prey *is about*
to be translated into Danish. She hopes to
broaden her repertoire to include the:

Pet Tawny Owl
American Vultures
and seven surviving species of the family
Catharrtedae.

Unwillingly and very seriously I found myself becoming more and more interested in *Birds of Prey*.

The boys wondered why I suddenly had so many books on birds. I wouldn't answer their questions.

Part Two

X

Of course, I dismissed Michael's accusations of James as cruel and ludicrous. James was the sweetest person I knew. He possessed compassion and a great empathy for others. But I did recognize that his roles in *Deadly Triplets* were cutting into a part of his mind in a dangerous way and making him miserable.

"Sometimes I feel that the triplets are victimizing me," he said. "They're usurping all my freedom; their thoughts of revenge are becoming my thoughts." He wrote that to me in a letter on the blue writing paper he used from Harrods. More and more he questioned whether he should be in the play and he suspected, somehow, it was having a profound and subtle effect on his life.

"I had no idea the hatred and sadness in this play were going to oppress me so. I'll be happy when the run is over. If I didn't have our talks, Suzanne, I couldn't do this play," he said. He held my hand tightly as we stood at the top of Primrose Hill in the snow and looked down over London.

"What a beautiful view," James said.

We walked in the snow down to Regents Park Road and looked in the antique shop windows. Christmas was coming. And James bought the boys an antique sailboat.

"They can sail this in Kensington Gardens," he said. We walked in the wonderful snow past the zoo all the way to Baker Street.

Sometimes we'd sit in the parlor and look out over the snowy garden listening to "I Shall Be Released" by Bobby Dylan. James gave me a copy of the album *Blonde on Blonde*.

I got a letter from Joe Papp encouraging me to hurry with the play I was writing for him. I was behind in my writing. I had abandoned my original idea and had started a play about James and me going to a film festival in Rome.

James and I talked again about Gina and whether she was still alive.

Christmas came. The boys and I went to the pantomime of Cinderella at the Palladium and to the auto show at Olympia. The house was filled even more with brass toy soldiers and painted train cars and games . . . one called Bezique and a miniature roulette wheel. We put a big tree in their room downstairs and played endless Christmas songs on their red and blue plastic record player while we ate Hovis bread and butter and drank hot chocolate.

That winter James and I continued our walks in the snow. He in a navy blue overcoat from Mr. Fish and I in my fashionable fake fur. Often James would say that with my masses of auburn hair and violet eyes I should be an actress. Even the English poet Adrian Mitchell had written a poem about my eyes.

We walked in the English winter twilight.

"Why do you continue to say you think Gina might be alive?" I asked him.

"It's just a feeling. You never really heard anyone say she's dead except the Shirer's secretary. Suzanne, do you know where Shirer is?"

"He died several years ago. I remember once when Antonia was interviewed in *Women's Wear Daily* she mentioned it . . . the fact that her father was no longer living."

"I still feel perhaps something happened . . . something pretty terrible and they took Gina away," he wrote in a letter that I kept with his other letters and a still photograph of him in *The Aristocrat* in the Victorian letter box I had bought on Portobello Road.

"I will help you find Antonia Shirer," he said as we walked along Chalcot Road. "You must get to the bottom of this for your sanity. It's distressing you so. It's marred your stay in England. I'm worried about you. I really do believe that if you and Antonia Shirer were to meet after all these years you could make amends. She must tell you the truth about your mother. We will go together. I will get her address from Vicki." He held my hand and kissed me very tenderly.

But he seemed somber the following week when we were sitting backstage at the theatre waiting for him to go on. He smeared the stage blood on the front of his costume, his face reflective.

"I've heard more about Antonia. It seems she possesses a tremendous charm but she can also be very bitter and venomous even to her friends."

XI

I wrote in my list:

Madeline Renaud

Jean Louis Barrault

I went to Paris for two rehearsals and the opening of *The Heart of Alain Delon* at the Petit Odéon. The director and I took an enchanting walk in the Luxembourg Gardens and we talked about one of the themes of the play . . . the American being killed abroad.

I caught a terrible cold in the Paris hotel and left before the play opened. But I did meet Jean Louis Barrault and Madeline Renaud in the magnificent foyer. We talked a few moments.

I brought James a copy of *Paris Match* which he loves and some drawings the set designer had done of the play.

When I returned to London from Paris I got a second note from John Sharples:

Dear Miss Sand:

Could you please come around one afternoon

*about five? I have found some objects you might
like to see . . . an old day bed, a gown, and a
wheelchair. They were in the cupboard that leads
to the garden. I'm afraid it appears the day bed
may have been spattered with blood, as if
someone lying on it had been bleeding. Any
afternoon at tea time I am home.*

*Do you know about any accident that might have
occurred involving your mother?*

> *Faithfully yours,*
> *John Sharples*

When I went the next day to Old Brompton Road to find
him, the house was darkened and shuttered. I went again the
following day exactly at five o'clock in the afternoon and
rang the bell. Again the house was dark and no one answered.
In the heavy deep snow I took the 74 bus back up to Primrose
Hill, exhausted. Then when I returned home there was a letter
in the foyer that had been put into the mail slot.

It was in a small pale gray envelope. I was puzzled be-
cause the letter had to have been delivered by a messenger, but
it didn't have a special delivery stamp. In fact the postmark
was hardly discernible. The letter said:

Dearest Suzanne:

*I am writing to you from Ireland. It is not true
what they told you. I need you. Help me.*

> *Your mother,*
> *Gina*

For the moment I decided against telling James.

"I do have Antonia's addresses now," James said one afternoon as we walked along the King's Road. "One in Los Angeles and one in Rome, where I'm told she is now. What I've been thinking is that we could go to Rome next month."

The conversations James and I were having were finding their way into another play. In the meantime the Royal Court decided to do *The Heart of Alain Delon* as soon as their new experimental theatre, Upstairs at the Court, opened.

It had been bothering me where I had seen Michael before the night of *Deadly Triplets*. I mentioned this one day to James.

"Probably you saw him the night he played the King in *Triplets*."

"You never mentioned that, James."

"Possibly because I was so furious with him. I don't know how he talked Victor into letting him do the role that night. I came out of my dressing room and there he was. But he takes great delight in that sort of thing. He feels he was an actor before I was. It's true I did follow in his footsteps. I wanted to be a writer. Anyway he feels it's his right to do that sort of thing. He played the King that night then just vanished. I think he was over here from New York talking to a movie producer."

My state of mind was such that I hardly realized that I was losing the Lennon project. The only moments of tranquillity that I had were the moments spent with the boys walking in the snow on Primrose Hill, listening to music on their red plastic phonograph with the blue handle, eating fish and chips from the shop on Regent's Park Road.

56

"Can we go see *Oliver?*" they asked. Again we went to Leicester Square to the movies.

I was beset with the thought: could there be a possibility that Gina was alive even though the postmark on the letter was 1944?

XII

I didn't hear from Michael, but one night when the boys were watching *The Saint* I saw him playing the role of a German spy. My mind was on Michael a great deal. I learned from Ann that he had appeared in *Room at the Top* and a couple of British thrillers; also I learned that both James and Michael had gone to Harrow. Another night he was on *The Saint*. He played a moody scientist; as I watched, I thought the lines in his face are harsher. He lacks the romantic aura that James possesses. He seemed always to be thinking, studying. James's face was a rush of emotions. Michael spoke evenly. James spoke feverishly then lapsed into silence.

James told me that he heard The Theatre had started rehearsals of a new version of *The Lennon Project* on the same day I received in the mail three photographs from Sharples . . . with no return address, only his imprint:

Sharples
South Kensington
London

on the back of each photo. The color photographs were of a steel wheelchair, a very white nightgown, a pale green day bed with faded splotches that appeared to be blood.

I went several times to Old Brompton Road searching for Sharples but the house was still shuttered.

My British literary agent said she had no information on the progress of the Lennon project. That day there was a photograph of the Beatles in India on the front page of *The Times*.

I met again with the man from Filmways. He asked me did I have any ideas for a movie. I told him I wasn't sure.

"What about this list of famous people that I keep reading about that you keep? Could that be developed?"

"I don't know. That's a hobby . . . my diversion."

"Think about it, Miss Sand." As I got up to leave he said, "It's amazing, you have violet eyes. And your coloring is beautiful. Is one of your parents Ethiopian?" I told him I didn't know who my parents were.

"With your coloring," he paused, "you could be in the film."

One morning James phoned to say that he and Vicki were having a party on Sunday.

"Vicki's very anxious to meet you."

Although it was early March, it was a beautiful Sunday. I put on my mauve print dress, with a mauve shawl that I had bought at Thea Porters and my white wool coat. Usually I took the Underground to Little Venice, but I decided to take the boat from the zoo. The boat stopped right in front of the huge white house that faced the canal.

James was standing at the doorway, a drink in his hand. He kissed my cheek.

"Suzanne, I've been waiting for you." He looked very tense. He led me past a cavernous drawing room where people were seated talking.

"Oh, I saw your play in New York. I loved it," someone said when we passed in the foyer hung with an oriental tapestry. Flowers were everywhere on stands and even on the floor. James said I must come upstairs and talk to Vicki.

"Suzanne, Vicki is upstairs refusing to come down," he said. "We planned this party. But she's angry because I invited Suzannah. She's jealous of anyone I've worked with. Please, can you go up and talk to her?" From the drawing room I could hear "MacArthurs Park" by Richard Harris.

He left me at the bottom of the stairs. As soon as I reached the second floor of the house I saw the dark green bedroom, the walls lined in paisley, shuttered windows that overlooked a fish pond in the garden. Vicki Eyre lay on the bed, smoking a cigarette. She wore a dazzling silver embroidered dress. She had a pale face beneath heavy make-up and thick dark brown hair cut severely in a geometric design. The room smelled of Paco Rabanne perfume. As soon as I came into her sight, she spoke.

"You're Suzanne Sand . . . what a lovely mauve dress." Beside her bed was a table crowded with photographs.

"I've been longing to meet you. I knew James was seeing you. But, of course, James never introduces me to anyone." She beckoned for me to sit in a highback chair.

"You do have violet eyes and auburn hair," she laughed. "You really do. I had read that in *Vogue*."

"And I heard from one of my dearest friends in New York

that your play was such a brilliant exploration of mixed identity. I do want to see it." Then, suddenly, she started to cry.

"I can't come downstairs. I've told James I don't want all these women he's had affairs with in this house. And what did he do? He invited one. I know they had an affair when they worked together. I know it." Among a group of photographs in the paisley behind the bed was one of Vicki on the cover of *Vogue,* in the fifties. She had been beautiful. Now her face was ashen and bloated from too much liquor.

Just then James burst into the room. He looked extraordinarily handsome that afternoon in a gray suit.

"I've sent them all home, Vicki."

"Oh, James," she tried to pull him to her.

"Yes, all of them. The party is over. Are you happy?"

And it was. James and I went downstairs. He called me a taxi. As we waited for the taxi the guests were scattering outside on the walk. I recognized an American novelist who lived in Switzerland, an actor from the Royal Court, and the American model Penelope Tree. They scattered down Maida Avenue, talking in the afternoon sun.

"I have something for you," James said. He disappeared down a flight of stairs and when he returned he gave me a pot of violets.

In three weeks I got a letter from Michael:

East 73rd Street, New York City

My dear Suzanne,

Please forgive me for behaving so badly when I called you from Heathrow. I don't know what on

earth possessed me to accuse James of such a
crime. Actually, I'm very worried about him and
must have been in a temporary state of madness
in order to suggest such a thing. Please forget
everything I said.

Yours,

Michael

The following week I got one more letter from Michael that began . . . poor James, he's been through so much . . . and went on to apologize for his "madness" once more.

For a while James seemed less agitated. He told me that he felt my writing was suffering and I mustn't let that happen. I had never told him about my visits back to Old Brompton Road. He made me read him pages of my new play.

"Suzanne, you are so brilliant. I wish I had something I could do really well."

Often we talked about the war that raged in Vietnam and we went to a demonstration against the war in Trafalgar Square. And there was also a lot of talk about the musical *Hair*, which was coming to London. It seemed that people were to appear nude on the stage.

Even though Michael had written me those letters, I heard from Ann that he had been at dinner parties all over London saying he feared James was becoming unbalanced and even dangerous.

"Is this true?" she asked.

"Of course not. But he is under a strain."

I was so preoccupied that I hardly realized I had lost the Lennon project. I hadn't wanted to mention it to Ann; but it had seemed since Michael appeared in *Deadly Triplets* that James's performance in the play had changed. It was hard to say whether or not he had been influenced by Michael's interpretation of the roles or whether he had changed his mind about the essence of the play. Before Michael's performance James had portrayed the triplets as very sympathetic victims who had been betrayed and duped by their uncle and then killed to gain power. The triplets had an innocence that made their ultimate revenge on the uncle, even though it was only in his dreams, gratifying. But something seemed to have changed in James's mind. In the way that he portrayed the triplets now it was the uncle, who craved their position and wealth, who seemed sympathetic. Because I had never acted on the stage, it was difficult for me to crystallize exactly how he had done this. But there was no doubt Michael's performance had changed how James saw the characters. And, too, the letters he wrote to me about his experiences on stage were more violent.

I had heard that during the few days Michael had rehearsed *Triplets* they had been at odds but that Michael had insisted James come to the rehearsal to advise him and critique what he was doing. They had gotten into a bad quarrel and James had pushed Michael.

"That's only natural. They're brothers," Victor Hamilton said.

Deadly Triplets closed. And a play by Edward Bond opened. Hamilton, the director of the Court, said he was interested in commissioning me to do a piece for their new little theatre, Upstairs at the Court. I began to think perhaps I could do something based on James's and my conversations about Fellini.

I hadn't heard any more from Michael but according to Sarah Constable Maxwell, whom I saw on the King's Road in Chelsea one afternoon, Michael's success in *Deadly Triplets* had made him reconsider living in New York and she had heard he was possibly coming back to live in England. His performance had been reviewed in several magazines and now he had been offered the role of Constantine in *The Seagull* at Nottingham.

XIII

It turned out that Michael had come back to England and was in Nottingham doing *The Seagull*. He sent a message by Sarah that he hoped I could see his performance. I wanted to talk to him: wanted him to tell me why he had changed his mind about James. I called him and said I was coming the next day on the afternoon train to Nottingham. Michael was in the lobby of the theatre waiting for me. He smiled.

"I have to go to rehearsal now," he said, "but I have a place for you to stay and we'll all have dinner after the play."

Michael was a superb Constantine. I cried when he shot himself. It was clear that he possessed power and great complexity as an actor. He had me seated next to him at dinner at the local restaurant. Most of the cast from the Chekov play was there. I still felt anxious not having had a moment alone with him: the conversation at dinner was so general and light that I doubted if I would be able to bring up the subject of James at all.

"Did you enjoy the play?"

"Oh, yes, *The Seagull* is one of my favorite plays, and my favorite of Chekov's. And you were really a tragic, touching Constantine."

"Thank you, Suzanne."

"Your performance had such depth."

"It means a lot to me that someone as observant as you would say that." He paused. "You know one of the reasons I wanted to see you was to apologize for that foolish phone call I made from Heathrow. I was upset and something terrible had happened that day."

"I understand, Michael."

"Did James mention it to you?"

"No, I don't believe he ever mentioned anything terrible happening on the day that you left for New York."

"Well in any case that was why I behaved so badly. You know James has always been terribly high strung." For a moment he almost seemed to forget me as he talked. "And he wasn't at all prepared for the success of *The Aristocrat*. You know he'd only had one or two roles in films. And at age 28 to be suddenly deluged with all the attention he's gotten, all the offers to be in American films."

Michael was somber.

"You know I love my brother very much and taking over his role in *Deadly Triplets* made me realize it more than ever, saying the words he said every night, using his dressing table, I even used his tattered marked script. ... The sense of struggle that he felt trying to articulate that role became a part of my struggle."

It was clear to me that night that Michael loved James very deeply.

I said I understood how his concern for James had made him suspicious of Vicki and that I had seen a lot less of James in the past weeks although he still sent me books on Italian films, a passion we shared. And we still talked on the phone.

"He's withdrawn from everyone but he's very fond of you." Michael poured me another glass of wine. Around us in the restaurant I could hear the actors talking about how this Chekov production compared to the Chekov production at the Royal Court of *The Three Sisters,* a while back. They all agreed how beautiful Marianne Faithfull had been.

"And I can tell you're fond of him," Michael smiled. I realized that night that he dressed very often as James dressed, in a navy blazer, Turnbull Asser shirt, and tie and gray flannels. Although Michael's hair was darker than James's, on that night he had combed it exactly as James wore his hair, to the side and falling on his forehead. Suddenly he leaned forward, taking my hand, almost an identical gesture to James's.

"You know, he's become increasingly withdrawn and unhinged . . . he tried to kill himself last night."

The room became a blur and I ran from the table. Somehow in the darkness I reached the Nottingham railway station. On the train to London I could think of only one thing: I had to see James. As the train sped to London, I realized how much I loved him.

Our talks about Gina and his work had made me closer to him than I had ever been to anyone: his concern for solving the mystery of Gina's death and his confidences about his fears made him dear to me. James, James, I must see you. I must help you.

Arriving in the station at two o'clock in the morning I took a taxi out to Little Venice. In the darkness it seemed to take forever as the taxi went along the narrow canal to the large white mansion. I went up the path that was enclosed in shrubbery and rang the bell. For a while there was silence. Through the long windows I could see a dim light. Finally the door opened and Vicki stood before me dressed in an embroidered long silk gown. She led me into the cavernous drawing room that smelled of incense.

I told her I had been in Nottingham and had seen Michael, and he had said that James had tried to kill himself and I wanted to see him.

"I understand your concern, Suzanne, dear, but James is fine now." In the dim light she looked much older than she had on the Sunday of the party with her harsh Sassoon hair cut, white face powder, and heavy dark eye make-up. She wore a heavy Paco Rabanne perfume. She appeared to just have come in. We sat on the chairs near the piano.

"What happened?"

"He simply took some pills and liquor." Her mind seemed far away. "But we were able to get him to the hospital on time."

"Why? Why?"

"I don't know. There doesn't seem to be a reason. I've given it a great deal of thought. He has everything a person could want . . . success . . . adoration. But he's at odds with it all . . . things I had so briefly when I was a model before I married . . . then I didn't understand how important they are."

Through the doorway I could see her evening coat thrown over the bannister on the stairs. I couldn't help but wonder where she had been.

"Suzanne, dear, the children's nurse and I got James to the hospital on time. He's fine now. But he's not here at the moment. He's in Hampshire. He wanted to go down to see Nancy Constable Maxwell. You know Sarah's aunt is practically like a mother to him and one of his dearest friends. Now let me get you a drink. Really, Suzanne, there's no need to worry. I'm sure he'll call you. James feels very close to you."

She brought me a chilled vodka and I sat silently in the moonlit room and drank it.

"You know this isn't the first time," she said.

"The first time?"

"That he's tried to kill himself."

"We're never going to be happy," she went on. "I know he wishes he'd married Sarah Constable Maxwell, you know they were engaged when James and I met." Moonlight from the back windows that faced the garden covered the cavernous room in a veil-like light. On a small marble table lay James's blue writing paper that he bought from Harrods and upon which he had written me letters, letters that talked about the experiences he often had on stage.

"Would you like another drink?"

"No, nothing. I think I'll go now." I felt exhausted and confused.

"Can you stay a moment. There's something I've learned." She stared at me intently, her dark eyes turning darker.

"I was amazed when I recently found out that I have been hearing about you for years from Antonia."

"James told me you are friends."

"She's one of my dearest friends. We were models together in New York. And for years I've been hearing about this Suzanne who was her stepsister for three years and how beautiful she was and how her mother loved this Suzanne so. I find it amazing that that is you."

"Yes, it is."

"We write each other constantly. She lives in Italy. I've told her that I met you. As a matter of fact she was here in London several weeks ago. No one really knows what she's been through. People only see this glamorous surface when they see Antonia. She never got over the accidental shooting of her mother . . . a terrible thing for a girl of fifteen."

"Was Gina shot?" This was the second time this evening that I felt almost bludgeoned about the head. I could not believe what I heard.

"I thought you knew that."

"No, I knew nothing."

"Antonia accidentally shot Gina . . . something she's never forgiven herself for."

"I never really knew what happened."

"That's all I know. Except she was hurt badly. And lived for some time afterward."

I started to cry. All these years I had been trying to piece it together, my trip to Old Brompton Road . . . I couldn't stop crying.

"Suzanne, I'm sorry. I had no idea you didn't know that. They took her to Ireland. How long she lived there I don't know."

"Although I only lived with Gina three years I think of her as my mother. I was five when they adopted me. She was the first person who I really felt loved me and of course soon after I was adopted she and Shirer separated and Antonia was with her father a lot so Gina and I spent a lot of time together. They told me she was dead."

"I am sorry," she said, "that I am the one to tell you this. I really am."

I wanted to leave. Vicki called me a taxi: the light was coming up over Primrose Hill as I arrived home. The boys were sleeping amid a clutter of trains, puzzles, and games. I kissed them goodnight. The baby sitter, a young drama student, was asleep on a cot near them. I went into the rose-colored bedroom and sat on the divan that was by the edge of the bed. I couldn't sleep. Suddenly I realized the boys were standing before me in their pajamas.

"Mommy, why are you crying?" they asked.

Although winter was almost over, snow had started to fall; the boys and I went for an early walk in Primrose Hill. They looked so beautiful bundled up in their blue jackets from Marks and Spencer, running up and down the hill. When we got home James called and said he wanted to see me as soon as he got back from Hampshire and that I mustn't worry, that he was fine.

"I want to talk to you about something important," he said. I sensed someone was listening to him, that someone was in the room with him.

"I must see you."

"I'll come and see you tomorrow, Suzanne."

And on that same day, for almost two hours, the boys were missing at the zoo. They were allowed to go to the zoo alone because we lived only three blocks away. The rule was that they would stay an hour. But after an hour they had not returned. I waited and waited, almost ready to call the bobbies. Finally I left a note for them and set out to search the zoo. As I came into view of the zoo gates, the boys came running up Primrose Hill breathless.

"We've found her," they said. "We've found Tessa. We saw her standing on the street and she got into a car and we ran and followed it all the way to Baker Street. We lost it. But we found Tessa."

When I look back, I realize I might have believed them but on that afternoon I was too distracted. Instead I paid no attention to their insistence that they had seen my sister Tessa. They had adored her so much. How wistful of them, I thought. How wistful and touching. I forgave them for running off down Primrose Hill pursuing a woman they thought was Tessa, my sister Tessa who had broken our hearts when she vanished from a dock at Southhampton, willfully leaving our family, five years earlier. And had never let us know her whereabouts. The boys knew Tessa from my old photographs of her.

The following night the adaptation of the Lennon books was to open at the theatre. The secretary called to say there would be tickets for me to come to the play and they hoped there were no hard feelings about my not continuing the project. After all, it was a story about a Liverpool boy's childhood. And even though Lennon had wanted me to continue, the producers thought otherwise.

That night James called. He was back in London. He said that he and Vicki were driving to Italy, that Vicki was positive a rest would improve his nerves and his spirits. He laughed that sweet little boy's laugh of his.

"I'm writing you a letter," he said. "But I will see you in a week."

I never received the letter and I never saw James again. Two days later he and Vicki were killed in an automobile accident in Italy, a crash so bad that their bodies were destroyed beyond all recognition. After their memorial service I took my children and went back to New York. I wanted to go home. I didn't know I had played a role in a well-planned crime.

Part Three

XIV

It was almost spring again. The boys and I lived on the Upper West Side on 76th Street near Columbus Avenue.

The play I had written for Joe Papp had opened at the Public Theatre. But all I could think of was James.

I still got the phone calls . . . only now there was static on the line as if the calls came from a foreign country. Sometimes I thought it might be Gina. Was she still alive? In Ireland?

Often I'd think I'd see James, walking down Central Park West going into the park in the twilight. Of course, I was mistaken. But often I'd run into the twilight calling James's name.

The boys and I took sailboats to Central Park, we bought toy soldiers at F. A.O. Schwartz, we saw the latest James Bond movie. But mostly I thought of James. I wrote letters to Michael at his London address, but he did not answer. The boys were back in school in New York and there was a great deal to take care of.

Sometimes after I put the boys to bed I would listen to Nino Rota and think of James. In the middle of the night I often found myself taking the faded letter from Gina and the four photographs out of the desk drawer, trying to make sense of them, unable to sleep, sensing there was an incomplete mystery within them. Often I felt that James was nearby trying still to help me solve the mystery of the events, including his own death, of that year in London. I felt this more and more with each passing night.

Filmways convinced me there was a film in my list of famous people, so I continued to write it. Romantic obsessions we will call them, he said.

My new piece at The Public Theatre was based on James's and my conversations about visiting Fellini in Rome. I made us characters who visit the set of *La Dolce Vita* and wind up in the movie. We disappear into *La Dolce Vita*, vanishing to reappear in that world anew. The piece seems to possess the mystery and intrigue of unresolved identity that seems to permeate my work.

But it also possesses music and romance and encompasses all the elements that we were robbed of by James's death.

I had had time since I left England to reflect that my desire to work on the Lennon Project and my desire to be interviewed by the press when I arrived in London had left me vulnerable and in some way perfect for some hidden elements behind James's death. It was something I sensed. I wrote Michael again to see if I could get more details of James's accident.

XV

Ann sent me two clippings that appeared in the newspaper after I left England, "Mystery Surrounds Death of British Film Star . . . was it suicide or accident?" And then another, "Mystery Continues to Surround the Death of James Eyre, who died in an automobile accident in Italy. There is still some confusion as to how the accident occurred and eyewitness accounts differ."

I knew I had to go back to London.

Suddenly one day Sarah Constable Maxwell phoned.

"I'm over here visiting my cousin. Can we meet?" We agreed to meet at Victor's Cafe on Columbus Avenue at 70th.

"I can't stop thinking of James," I said after we had ordered drinks.

"That picture of you in *Vogue* last month was so unhappy and today you look so pale," she said.

"I'll never get over James's death."

Silently for a few moments we sipped our drinks. She wore a lovely pale wool coat. Her blonde hair fell to her shoulders. There was a wistful quality about Sarah that I had always liked and trusted.

"Our family has been more distressed than ever."

"Is there something more that I don't know?" I asked.

"There still does seem to be some growing confusion because in Italy an eyewitness drove away and they've never been able to find him. I think it would have all been settled if it weren't for James's mother. She keeps raising these questions. You know, Suzanne, there is some doubt as to how they died . . . whether it was an accident. . . . A lot of people think James killed Vicki or that he may have committed suicide."

"I don't believe that."

She looked out of the glass enclosure of the restaurant.

"I knew you'd want to see them. I brought these clippings."

She opened her purse and pulled out some newspaper clippings. And at the same time started to talk almost absently.

"I always believed his relationship with Vicki would end badly. I knew her love for James would somehow eventually strangle him. He feared her and felt great anguish over her jealousy. She had captured one of the most idolized young actors in London and it had come after years of isolation and living in the shadow of . . . that director who left her. I wrote him letters and tried to warn him. She'd often follow him on the street. Did you know that? Often when he'd come to visit my aunt, Vicki would come to Hampshire, follow James, take a room in the local inn. She came down to Hampshire the night after he tried to kill himself."

She handed me the clippings.

"These were in the *Express* last week."

I looked at the clippings.

"Letters to American Writer That Have Surfaced Indicate James Eyre's Emotional Problems."

I wondered how James's letters to me had reached the press.

"Has anyone from the newspaper phoned you?" she asked.

"No . . . ?"

The letters did not appear in print but just the information that there was a half dozen or so written to the American writer Suzanne Sand and they confirmed the fact that during James Eyre's performance in *Deadly Triplets* he had indeed suffered some kind of emotional crisis.

I knew I had to go to London. Sarah, gazing out the window, went on talking.

"Well, you know James spent a lot of time at our house in Hampshire. My Aunt Nancy adored him. They spent hours sitting in the chapel in our house talking. Being the star of *The Aristocrat* was one thing but to try to appear on the stage in such a strenuous role was too much for him. And you know the critics around London said that even though he excelled in *Aristocrat,* he was a weak actor. Things were very difficult for him. He was offered roles but he really lacked the drive and aggressiveness that his father expected of him. Aunt Nancy says James should have been a poet." When she lifted her head, I saw that she was crying.

"I was always sorry that James and I didn't marry. I was so in love with him. My aunt and his mother had it practically all planned out. But then he met Vicki."

We had coffee. Sarah said she was late for another appointment.

"Good-bye, Suzanne, I'm so glad we talked and I'm so looking forward to seeing your new play at the Public Theatre. You know sometimes I think James was really deeply in love with you," she paused.

"You know there's one more thing, John Sharples . . . the photographer was at a friend's house in the country and rather drunk and he kept talking about a hoax he and a friend had played. . . . I don't know why but something about it

79

made me think it had involved you because the last time I saw James in Hampshire he had said that he had just discovered someone had attempted to hurt a close friend of his badly through a very cruel and bizarre deception."

"I am coming to London," I said. "About John Sharples, that is something that perhaps one day I will talk about but not now." She hurried down Columbus Avenue. We waved good-bye.

So it really was true what I had long suspected, that Antonia and Sharples had faked the photo "clues" of Gina's death. I realized now more than ever that wherever Antonia was I still had her to fear. Of course, I could never prove this. So what could I do?

I understood now why James had been puzzled when he saw the picture of Gina and me. Because he realized, through his knowledge of film, that the Sharples photograph was an illusion done by trick photography: taking an old photograph of Gina and imposing a child on it was simple. The child I hoped was me was not me at all.

And of course, I realized this was true of the other photographs of the day bed with blood, the gown, the wheelchair . . .

As I walked home down Columbus Avenue I realized again that there had always been so much I had not known. Not until today while we were at lunch did I know that it was Michael who had introduced James to Vicki and that Vicki and Michael had been close friends before Vicki moved to London. Michael had known her when she was still married to the director. . . . It had been Michael who had encouraged Vicki to move to London. He felt a deep love for her but she was so desperately unhappy over her divorce that he had remained quiet about his feelings for her. And it had been

Michael who had introduced Vicki and James to each other. Sarah said that once in an outburst at a party Michael had said all these things to anyone who was listening which, of course, was very unlike him. It had been a party at Victor Hamilton's celebrating Michael's success in *Deadly Triplets*.

Michael, Michael. I almost thought of Michael now as much as I did of James. Why hadn't he answered my letters to him?

When I arrived back at the apartment there was a letter from a Mr. Crawley in London. It said that if I had occasion to be in London in the near future he would like to see me, that a client of his wanted very much to talk to me.

The boys would be on spring vacation in a week and would be going on a trip to California with their father. This was the ideal time to go to England. I wrote Ann and Robert to ask if I could stay with them.

XVI

I arrived in London just as the *Daily Express* was publishing more excerpts from James's letters to me.

From Backstage at The Court

Dear Suzanne:

I have written down entire scenes from the Frankenstein *play I saw in Amsterdam last winter in order to study them. The play has become a sign post of a personal dilemma that I sense exists in my life just beyond my consciousness, just as when I was twenty and read* The Brothers Karamazov, *and knew from that moment that there was a travail that existed between my father, my brother, and myself.*

And now I feel this production of Frankenstein *more than any other play except the play of* Crime and Punishment *that I saw in Paris is*

*informing me, far more than the play I am
appearing in* (Deadly Triplets).

The strange part is although I saw the
Frankenstein *play months ago I did not start to be
haunted by it until I started to work on* Deadly
Triplets. *It was during the rehearsal of* Triplets
*that I began having nightmares about the first
scene in* Frankenstein, *the scene of Walton seeing
the figure in the icy tundra.*

*Perhaps it is because I am exhausted from
working on* Deadly Triplets *and am vulnerable.*

On the second day in London I went to Crawley's law
office on Berkeley Square. A large expressionless man called
Crawley behind a desk thanked me for coming in then ques-
tioned me as to James's state of mind during my friendship
with him. He said that James's mother could have no peace of
mind about her son until she understood what had happened
to him the last months of his life.

"She would like to meet you."

I told Crawley I would be happy to see James's mother.

"She in no way blames you. Let me make that clear. But
it does appear that Michael told her that you were close to
James in those last months and naturally there is all this fuss
over the letters he wrote you. I hope you'll come. She suggests
I bring you to her house. You know she's one of my best cli-
ents . . . you know she's cousin to the Queen." He said he
would call in a day or so. He did call a few days later but said
that the meeting was postponed, that Lady Eyre wasn't feel-
ing well and had gone to her house on Elba.

By now fragments of two of the letters James had written to me had been published in the *Express*. When I called the paper I was told they had received the letters in the mail.

If only I could find Michael, I thought. Victor Hamilton said he wasn't at all sure where Michael "actually was." I called Bill Weldon and told him I wanted to see him.

Weldon invited me to come to Yorkshire for two days. We walked on the moors.

"I really wanted to find Michael Eyre," I said.

"Michael Eyre," he said "Well you don't have to look much further. He lives near by."

"Near here?"

"Yes, he came back from America several months ago. I must say he seems far happier than he was years ago; his hatred and jealousy of his brother seem to have waned: James's celebrity filled him with such darkness. You know he had been an actor long before James and was doing rather well at it. But then James became a star. It drove him mad. He went to America and tried to escape it. Nothing ever seemed to go really right for him. He never really got the recognition he craved until he replaced James for those few days in *Deadly Triplets*."

"Do you ever see him?"

"Oh never. He and his wife keep totally to themselves. You know he married recently. I never much cared for him, but after I saw him in *Triplets* I realized he was a far finer actor than James, although I adored James. I'm rewriting my play for Michael. You know he turned out to be immensely loyal. He went through the dreadful task of identifying what was left of Vicki's and James's bodies. His mother was distraught and his father was sick so it fell to him to deal with the official things that have to be taken care of when a person is killed in a foreign country. Of course, there was nothing left of the bodies to bury, but he had to organize the memorial service. I understand he's been a great comfort to his mother. And, of course, it all must have been especially horrid since Victoria was really the love of Michael's life."

"I never knew that." Again I realized so many, many mysteries about James, Vicki, and Michael had not been known to me. I understood I really had known very little about them.

"I understand he and Vicki became close again when he was here doing *Triplets* . . . poor Vicki. Her fear of losing James had driven her into such isolation and despair. But since Michael's recently married I guess he's gotten over all that."

"When did he marry?"

"I'm not sure. It was a few months ago in Italy or France."

The next day I went to Haworth and the Brontës' cottage, leaving Weldon to write.

When I returned to the cottage, Weldon said that he had sent a message to Michael that I was in Yorkshire and that he had invited us to tea. After Weldon finished his writing, we set out walking across the steep green moors. Even though it was summer, the weather was damp and cold. I pulled my violet knitted shawl close. I felt such a longing to see Michael, and yet I was afraid.

Although it was not quite six o'clock it had gotten quite dark.

"I've always felt badly that it was *Deadly Triplets* that sent James over the edge," Weldon said. "I liked James very much . . . he was such a sweet, romantic person."

Suddenly I felt exhausted; the walk was much longer than I had expected.

"I don't believe what so many people believe that he murdered Vicki. But those letters he wrote you that were published in the *Daily Express* did prove that murder was on his mind and he was unbalanced enough to kill his wife even if it meant killing himself or perhaps he hadn't planned to kill himself."

"I can never believe that James would murder," I said.

A very fine rain started. I wanted to hear the facts about Italy, about the accident, about where they had been in Italy. Only the sketchiest details had been in the paper. And yet I knew that Michael wouldn't tell me. By now I knew that whatever he did tell me would be very little. And that it would suit him in some way. Soon we came in view of a series of gray stone buildings. We walked down a hill toward them.

"That's the place," said Weldon.

At the bottom of the hill we passed several stone structures of various sizes. One appeared to be a barn. Weldon led me around the house to the front which faced the moors. The house was surrounded by a stone fence that enclosed a garden.

My heart caught when the door opened. I believed it was James. It is James. But it was Michael. He had dyed his hair the same blond of James's hair and he wore a navy blue suit very like the suit that James had worn when we had lunch that first day on Beauchamp Place. He looked almost identical to James. The sight of him made me breathless. He was most cordial.

"Come in, Bill. And Suzanne, I'm so happy to see you again. You're more beautiful than ever." He kissed both my cheeks. It is James, I thought. I knew James wasn't dead, not James, James listening to the music of Nino Rota, James holding my hand, James on the stage at the Royal Court, but it wasn't James, it was Michael.

"My wife won't be able to join us. She's not feeling well."

He led us to a very large room with books, drawings, and old furniture. We had tea in this large stone room. I felt cold and almost faint as James and Weldon discussed Weldon's new play he was writing for Michael. It would open at the Court in the winter. Michael seemed aware that I couldn't take my eyes off him.

"Suzanne, I'll always be grateful to you for being a friend to James. You were a comfort to him." He stood up and came and sat beside me on the dark velvet divan. "And I hear you're doing so well in America. I understand your new play got marvelous reviews."

"Michael, I must talk to you. I want to talk to you about what happened. Can I return tomorrow?"

"Tomorrow my wife and I are going to Malta, but when we return I will call you."

"Michael I must talk to you now. I want to know what happened in Italy. Please."

"Suzanne, it won't help, knowing sad details, believe me." Weldon took my arm. "Come, let's start back."

Michael smiled.

"Suzanne, I will call you the moment I return."

"You won't, " I said. "I know you won't."

Weldon gently guided me toward the door and into the garden. Michael followed us.

"Bill, see that she gets rest. I'm worried about her." He kissed me again on both cheeks. As we came down the path I glimpsed Michael's wife in the window hidden by a drapery.

We started through the gate and back around the house to the moors.

"I want to know what happened," I sobbed. "I want to know what happened."

By now I knew that Michael would not return from Malta before I left for New York and he didn't. I called the house in

Yorkshire several times after I returned to London but there was never any answer. I went back to New York.

That winter Michael opened in Weldon's new play. It was a big success.

Sarah Constable Maxwell sent me the reviews.

Critics said what a fine actor Michael Eyre was, and it was a pleasure to welcome him back after his years in America and that he had been sorely missed. He was acknowledged as having become, along with Scofield and Finney, one of the major actors in British theatre. Years from now he may fill Olivier's shoes, one review had said . . . his subtlety his mastery of characterization . . .

The following month Michael and Victoria were arrested for the murder of James Eyre.

XVII

Weldon wrote me that Michael's success had brought on a high emotional state. Then he started to lose control and suddenly on stage, in the middle of a scene, he would start to talk like James and then the laugh. It was as if James was saying the lines, and it was as if Michael's dreams had finally come true. He had become his famous brother. People thought it would pass, they thought James's death was obsessing him and that he would exorcise his brother's spirit. Instead, James's personality became stronger in Michael and his performance took on James's delicate lyricism, the boyish romanticism. Finally one night, in the middle of the performance, he stopped and came to the edge of the stage:

> *"They murdered me, you know, my*
> *brother Michael and Vicki . . . they*
> *plotted my death. . . . They murdered*
> *me, you know, my brother Michael*
> *and Vicki . . . "*

And then he resumed his performance.

Weldon said that *after* that a strange thing occurred, that when Michael was on stage, he performed as Michael, but *after* that night, whenever he was off stage, he was James. Of course, the most shocking part was that Vicki was alive and they had married. That had been her face I saw in the window that evening in Yorkshire . . . a face altered by surgery . . . the "accident," Michael's going to Italy, the stories of Vicki's death had all been a plan. Through Michael's relapse as James, it was learned how the accident had been faked.

Weldon said he had gone to see "Vicki," her face totally altered by plastic surgery. It was before she was arrested and as they sat in the dark maroon-colored bedroom overlooking the moors, she had told him: "Michael came to see me when he was in *Triplets,* it was a turning point for him. He had always cared for me and said he was saddened that I had fallen into such misery over James. My anguish made it easy for him to convince me that perhaps we could go somewhere and fake some sort of accident."

"We've both suffered so from his existence," he said. "I realized I could have a remarkable life too except that my hatred for James is consuming me."

"He asked me to marry him. He said that he had always loved me very much and had been heartbroken when James and I fell in love. Michael and I decided that we should use James's suicide attempts. We reasoned that if anything should happen to him, anything at all, that some people would suspect that James had taken his life, that it would be confusing and we would profit by the confusion. We would profit by his breakdown and profit by the existence of the letters he had written to Suzanne Sand which I had secretly read and copied before they mailed them. (Of course, it had been those letters which had "found" their way into the *Daily Express*.) Since James's breakdown in *Deadly Triplets* had been so public, we knew that a mystery would surround his death. I told one or two friends that I had begun to fear James . . . and I was beginning to think he might be dangerous. And before we went to Italy I even called his mother and wept that when we returned from our trip I wanted to show her copies of some letters he had written, in which murder was a constant preoccupation and perhaps I might be in danger and that I wanted to come and see her as soon as we came back to London. Of course, I knew she would become hysterical and that this hysteria would be helpful after the 'accident.' James's sense of danger had been very accurate. He sensed something was ghastly around him and that was the incredible part of his breakdown. He sensed my thoughts toward him. And that was why Michael befriended Suzanne Sand. Michael said we must always know what she's thinking."

"We knew that James had told her of his premonitions. You see, Weldon, we didn't really plan to murder him, at that time, but the letters to Suzanne, his breakdown, all provided us with an almost spontaneous, almost random, almost perfect opportunity for murder."

James's premonitions of "murder" and danger had been of his own, wrote Weldon.

XVIII

And now.

It is the day after John Lennon was murdered. I walk from 76th Street along Columbus Avenue in the December cold to 72nd and Central Park West. It is late afternoon.

A vast crowd is standing outside the Dakota apartment with candles and flowers. Some are singing the song "Imagine"; some are weeping. I remember Lennon sitting in the office near Grosvenor Square trying to keep me a part of the Lennon project. Someone gives me a flower.

Even though I know the hoax Antonia and Sharples played, I still can't help but wonder sometimes, is Gina still alive? And will Antonia continue to disturb my life?

I've never been back to London. But every time I hear *MacArthurs Park*, or *I Shall Be Released* or the music of Nino Rota or see a Fellini movie, I think of James . . . in the sun driving up Primrose Hill in his yellow Lotus. I think of him.

London

*Adam and Joe in front of No. 39,
the first house we lived in on
Chalcot Crescent, 1967*

*The boys in our garden at
No. 35 Chalcot Crescent, 1968*

Just before I left for London, 1966

Our block and No. 35 Chalcot Crescent twenty years later, 1988; many more cars, but everything else looks the same

Flyers for Sun *at the Royal Court Theatre, London, summer of 1969, and* Cities in Bezique *at the Public Theater, New York, winter of 1969*

THE THEATRE
UPSTAIRS

AT THE ROYAL
COURT
THEATRE
SLO 2554

SEASON OPENS JULY 15
BLIM AT SCHOOL................by   PETER TEGEL
& POET OF THE ANEMONES......by   PETER GILL
OVER GARDENS OUT..............by   ADRIENNE KENNEDY
SUN...................................by   HOWARD BRENTON
REVENGE
AND THE PEOPLE SHOW

...se are some of the plays you will be able to see in The
...eatre Upstairs over the next three months.
...l the plays are new, and all are by young writers who live in
...ondon, and will be closely involved in the production of their
...wn play.

...The list is not complete, and never will be. Certainly more
plays, events and late-night shows will be added to this pro-
gramme, sometimes at very short notice.

Details will be sent to you, and will appear in the press, and at
the theatre. Or ring us up, any time, at 730 2554.

New York Shakespeare Festival
PUBLIC THEATER

Adrienne Kennedy's

CITIES IN BEZIQUE

LIMITED ENGAGEMENT – NOW THRU MARCH 2

"BEATS ON THE MIND LIKE VERSE—
ENCAPSULATES THE IMAGINATION LIKE A MOVIE . . ."

"Cities in Bezique—two plays by Adrienne Kennedy—have no beginning, no middle, no end—and yet they wrap around the mind like strange tendrils.

". . . the language is wild . . . beats on the mind like verse—encapsulates the imagination like a movie . . . amazing and poetic."   —Clive Barnes, New York Times

"A REMARKABLE THEATRICAL ACHIEVEMENT . . . THERE CAN BE
NO DOUBT OF ITS STUNNING PHANTOMSTREWN POWER.

"Adrienne Kennedy has a fascinating imagination, and her eerie Cities in Bezique is a remarkable theatrical achievement. As drama, it is cloudy, obscure and frequently bewildering but there can be no doubt of its stunning, phantomstrewn power.

"Both (plays) are filled with 'her strange gift for lyric fascination . . . the staging is imaginative, the performances excellent."   —Richard Watts, New York Post

"AN ASSAULT ON THE SENSES

". . . an assault on the senses with director Gerald Freedman using his actors, Ming Cho Lee's scenery, Theoni V. Aldredge's costumes, Martin Aronstein's lighting and John Morris' affecting music to expose us to a moody, fearsome picture of life in the black world."   —Lee Silver, Daily News

"EXTRAORDINARY SHORT DRAMAS

"Mrs. Kennedy's extraordinary short dramas, compounded as they are of poetry, terror, and wit, demand and hold one's unflagging attention."   —New Yorker

"THE OWL ANSWERS IS THE BEST NEW PLAY OFF OR FOR THAT MATTER
ON BROADWAY THIS YEAR."   —WNEW

TICKETS NOW ON SALE THRU MARCH 2
Telephone reservations. Call 677-6350
Tues., Wed., Thurs. eves. at 8:30 and Sun. at 3:00 and 7:30: $3.75
Fri. at 8:30 and Sat. at 5:00 and 9:00: $4.75
Youth Tickets—all performances: $1.75

NEXT AT THE PUBLIC THEATER
Vladimir Nabokov's

Funnyhouse of a Negro
at the Petit Odéon, Paris,
spring of 1968

The front jacket of The Lennon Play,
published by Jonathan Cape
Publishers, 1968

A Theatre Journal

In 1981 when I was teaching at Berkeley, I decided to write a piece entitled *People I've Met in the Theatre*. I belonged to a group of writers who met on Sunday evenings on College Ave. One evening they asked me about winning the Obie. They wanted to hear about off-Broadway in the sixties. They wanted to hear about my meeting the Beatles during my stay in London, one of them said what a "glorious past" you've had. I remembered a film producer in London had asked me to do a screenplay on my life there, as a Black woman in 1966–69. I had been unsure about that, and had declined, but had often regretted I had not at least tried.

So now sitting on the Berkeley campus in the spring at the Faculty Club, in a lovely room facing a redwood tree and a creek, I started the first sketches about off-Broadway, choosing what I felt to be exciting moments in my life. They concerned *Funnyhouse of a Negro,* my Obie-winning play. One of the reasons I chose sketches was a book I read when I was twenty-one, by Daniel Blum, called *Famous People in the American Theatre.* How I had loved the short, dense paragraphs about the actors and actresses accompanied by a black-

and-white photo. How I had longed to be in that book. Just as my diaries had always been filled with scenes of my life presented in short passages, now these sketches took the same form. I started with the time of the first workshop of *Funnyhouse* and continued with the days that led to my trip to London.

Edward Albee

When I joined Albee's workshop, January 1962, I submitted my play *Funnyhouse of a Negro* as a writing sample to get into the class. You were to mail or bring your play to the Circle-in-the-Square. My husband took it down to Bleeker Street on his way to work. He relayed a message that a secretary had said that the people who would be selected to be in the class would soon receive a phone call. Finally after several weeks someone called. He said his name was Michael Kahn. "Edward Albee liked your play very much, you have been selected to be in the workshop." There were about thirteen of us that went up the long dark steps to the room above the Circle.

Albee was wearing a tweed suit and seemed shy and frightened. In a muted voice he read from his notes about what our playwriting class was to consist of. Each person was required to have a play done in workshop. Outside the wind blew the Circle-in-the-Square sign which still hangs there today. He invited the class to a rehearsal of the *Sandbox* at the Cherry Lane. During that rehearsal he went up on the stage and quietly spoke to the actors; there was a hole in his sweater, it gave him the air of a struggling writer. Michael Kahn was the Circle's brilliant young director. It was his job to cast the workshop productions. My play was to be in April. Michael had mentioned the possible casting of Diana Sands, Yaphet Kotto, and others. But during the winter, I became frightened. My play seemed far too revealing and much to my own shock, I had used the word "nigger" throughout the text. I decided to drop out of the class.

I arrived early at what I thought would be my last class. Since the workshop productions had started, the class had moved down into the theatre. Edward Albee was in the theatre alone.

"Mr. Albee," I said, "I've decided to drop the class." He stared straight into my face with his exceptional eyes.

"Oh," he said. "It's your decision. But don't you want to see your play performed? It is a chance to see your characters on the stage."

"My play is too revealing," I said. "I'm embarrassed to have it done. The other plays so far are not as revealing."

He stuck his hands into his pockets, came closer to me and stared. His gaze was hypnotic.

"Do you see that stage?" he said, glancing at the Circle's theatre in the round.

"Yes."

"Well, do you know what a playwright is? A playwright is someone who lets his guts out on the stage and that's what you've done in this play." I didn't know what to say. That was the point. I didn't want my guts let out in front of the whole class. I stepped back and started toward the door.

"It's your decision," he said. He didn't smile or move but only continued to look at me with his hypnotic eyes.

Michael Kahn

We were rehearsing my play at the Actors' Studio. Michael told me that several theatre people would be there to see it. At the first performance three weeks earlier, the play had been so controversial that regulars who had missed it had been invited: among them Rip Torn, Geraldine Page, Harold Clurman. Although Michael was many years younger than I was, he was experienced in the theatre and attempted to be reassuring. It was Michael's connection to the studio that gave me this opportunity.

The idea of doing a play that theatre people were coming to see and were going to comment on afterward, while I, again, sat in front on a single chair, made me sick. During one of the last rehearsals I felt so frightened that I ran outside and sat on the steps. Michael came outside and tried to talk to me. He said something to the effect of, you shouldn't worry darling. I was in tears. "Don't call me darling," I said.

"Everyone in the theatre says darling," he said quite nonplussed. "It's a theatrical expression." He went on attempting to paint a reassuring picture.

People in these first three production of *Funnyhouse*, the first at Circle-in-the-Square, the second and third at Actor's Studio, were Diana Sands, Fran Bennett, Lynne Hamilton, Yaphet Kotto, and Andre Gregory, all of whom became immensely successful.

At the Studio Molly Kazan was the head of the Playwright's Unit. After the play was performed it was the practice of the Unit members to demolish the playwright. Although I was thoroughly demolished, they asked me to join the Unit.

In Berkeley that spring of 1981 I wrote several sketches about the two years after the workshop and the off-Broadway production of *Funnyhouse* and read them to my Sunday group. But they continued to ask me about London. I tried hard to recapture the months that led to my leaving New York in the fall of 1966.

102

My father now lived in Georgia with his second wife. When he sent me photographs of himself he seemed older. How could this man in a photograph with a "second wife" be my father? How I needed then to recall Emerson's "nothing in the Universe is fixed." But I'm not sure I did.

Often I thought of Lady MacBeth: She could not get the blood from her hands. Calpurnia, she was Caesar's gentle wife, I thought of Caesar and Brutus and Cassius and the lines, "if we do meet again then we shall smile, if not then this parting was well made." I thought of Lear, betrayal, Ophelia: she went mad, Rilke (*Elegies*), St. John Perse, *Dubliners*, Stephen Dedalus. I still stared at Martha Graham's photograph of the dance *This Is My Letter to the World*.

Divorced, I was often alone with the children. When Joe came to see them, I'd weep when he left. Often I thought of my blue evening gown for the opening night of *Funnyhouse* or the room of white flowers at the party in Albee's house on Tenth Street. Some people who were on my mind were Richard Burton (the film life of Edwin Booth, *Prince of Players*), Michael Caine as Harry Palmer in *The Ipcress File, Darling*, Dr. Zhivago (Omar Sharif), and still Dylan Thomas's *Adventures in the Skin Trade*. For a few months I lived on Bedford Street blocks away from St. Vincents Hospital where Thomas died. I had once run there in the middle of the night when my son Adam was burning with fever. Yes, *Adventures in the Skin Trade* where Martha jumped from the window and thought she was flying, "but Martha was not flying." And Djuna Barnes's *Nightwood*. I had once stared into her courtyard near Patchin Place, and always Dante's *Purgatory*, Fellini's

Senso, Visconti's *The Leopard,* incessantly Bergman's *Wild Strawberries,* and Fellini's *La Dolce Vita* (Steiner killed himself and his children). Soon I would go to London and live in Primrose Hill and think of Marks and Spencer, Regent's Park Road, the Wax Museum. My son Joe had Lennon's nonsense books and the children constantly sang Beatles songs. Often I sat among their toys reading the nonsense books, *A Spaniard in the Works* and *In His Own Write.*

I thought perhaps I could make a play of these stories. I told Gillian Walker at Circle-in-the-Square. She was a producer who had come to see *The Owl Answers* at the De Lys and had been talking to Ted Mann about my work. They wanted me to write a play for the Circle. She immediately wrote to Lennon's publisher, Jonathan Cape. At the same time by now I had a Rockefeller Grant. I decided to put my furniture in storage and go to England. For a few days before we left I stayed in the empty studio atop the Dakota that Gillian often let her friends use. It was there I started *The Lennon Play,* dramatic scenes from Lennon's stories.

Years later when Lennon was murdered outside the Dakota I would walk in the winter rain and stand before the dark massive apartment on the street with a crowd carrying candles and flowers singing "Imagine." But for now, amid the green turrets and gothic roof, I sat in the tiny, dim studio piecing together early scenes of *The Lennon Play.* I didn't know that by the time these pages reached the stage at the National Theatre I would have lived some of the most wondrous and enchanting months of my life.

When Gillian came in early in the evening she invited us down to her apartment for one of her very popular, crowded dinners. On one of these evenings she hurriedly prepared for a big formal evening. Her escort would soon pick her up to go to Truman Capote's ball.

I was to go to England in three days, two days, one. I wanted to leave New York very much.

Those were just a few of the sketches I read to my Berkeley group on Sunday spring evenings. They laughed and were often delighted by them. So during the week after classes and walking through beautiful Faculty Glade I continued writing, sitting at the open window facing the redwood tree. My Sunday group wanted to know more, they wanted to know about London, about meeting the Beatles and working for a while on the "Lennon project." I remembered now that many people often had asked me this so the English sketches began to dominate the material. And it was as though these people had existed in a dream. The moments I had seen them returned to me in brief passages.

As I wrote in *People Who Led to My Plays,* I had first gone to London with my husband and son in 1961. We traveled on the *Queen Elizabeth.* Queen Victoria would become a character in *Funnyhouse of a Negro* and long passages of *The Owl Answers* were inspired by a trip to the Tower of London. We had gone on to Africa. But several months later I had returned to London for three weeks with my son, after leaving Africa. I stayed the entire time in a room I found through American Express, on Old Brompton Road. It overlooked a dark square garden fenced in by an iron gate. You lit the fire with shillings. The city in February, the early darkness, walks in the rain excited me. It made me feel that just beyond that darkness was a completed person, a completed writer, a completed life. I felt the city held a key to my psyche. And apart from literature and my constant interest in British writers I felt too these were the people who had colonized my West African ancestors. What were these people like?

Long ago my mother had told me her father's family came from England. Anything about England had fascinated: scenes on Christmas cards, *A Christmas Carol,* the Brontës, Churchill, the War, the Bombing of England, England in World War II movies, Olivier and Vivian Leigh and, of course, *Hamlet, Tale of Two Cities, Mill on the Floss.* My public-school education had been totally dominated by English literature.

And, of course, the issue of race. As I had explored in *Funnyhouse* through Sarah's obsession with Queen Victoria, who were these people who had conquered the world?

In Berkeley I walked constantly through the eucalyptus trees and stared at the bay and wrote. My friends in my writers' group loved the short portraits of people. So I continued pages and scenes.

Joe Losey

The last evening I was in New York, Diana Sands came to visit. I had run into Diana two days before at the Circle-in-the-Square. When I told her I was going to London, she said, "I want to give you several names and addresses." She had just returned from London having starred in *The Owl and the Pussycat* in the West End and hoped we could interest someone in my plays with her in them. Diana had starred in the first workshop production of my play at the Circle-in-the-Square and her performance was a big factor in the intense interest the play aroused. "Joe Losey is the first person I want you to call," she said. "He's one of my best friends. Please give him a copy of your plays. Maybe he'll consider them for a movie."

I arrived in London on a Thursday and called Joe Losey's house. A woman answered who said, "I'm his wife, Patricia." I conveyed my message from Diana telling her Diana hoped

Joe Losey would read my plays. "Why don't you drop them off Monday morning about eleven o'clock." She said they lived in Chelsea off the King's Road. When I arrived Monday I was met by a very friendly woman in her thirties. She was talkative and asked me a great deal about myself. She told me she used to work with Joe Losey but now that they were married, she no longer did. She showed great enthusiasm for Diana Sands and said she knew Joe Losey would read the plays immediately. Before I left, she asked me did I realize that *The Servant* was filmed at the house across the street. I left the plays. A few days later when I returned to my hotel in Queensgate Terrace from a walk the desk clerk told me a messenger had delivered a package to me. The package was my plays. Inside the manuscript was a note on white paper. It said.

Dear Mrs. Kennedy,

I read these plays only because Diana Sands suggested it but I'm not attracted to this material at all.

Joe Losey

Kenneth Tynan

A director and I met at Tynan's house on Thurlow Square. After a tour of the house to which they had just moved, his wife, Kathleen Tynan, the director, and I set out walking to find a restaurant and finally settled on a tiny place with a counter and stools. Several bottles of A-1 sauce were on a tray on the counter. Seated next to him, I expected Kenneth Tynan to embark on the history or an analysis of the English Theatre. He spent his entire lunch describing the many uses of A-1 sauce on English food and his love of the movie *From Russia with Love*.

James Earl Jones

The day I moved to Primrose Hill from a small hotel in Queensgate Terrace, I got a phone call.

"Hello Adrienne, this is James Earl Jones."

We had met when Ellen Holly had introduced us backstage at a production of *Macbeth* that Joe Papp had done in Washington Square Park. I remembered his unusually intense brown eyes. "I'm in London," he said, "and I don't know anyone." My new friends all wanted to meet him. Ricki Huston invited a group to her house on Maida Vale. Jimmy was preparing to do a movie in France with the Burtons, a Graham Greene novel. His mention of the Burtons reminded me of my old teen-age obsession with Elizabeth Taylor. "Jimmy," I said, "when you're making the movie with the Burtons, could you get me Elizabeth Taylor's autograph?" "I will," he said matter-of-factly. He came to London several times while filming the movie, once bringing with him a man who was writing a book on Africa. Finally at the end of the summer Jimmy came to London again. Would he be going back to France?

"The filming is over," he said.

"Did you ever get Elizabeth Taylor's autograph?"

"No," he said apologetically. "No, I wanted to because I knew you really wanted it, but I felt funny asking her for an autograph."

Alex Haley

The man James Earl Jones brought to visit me in Primrose

Hill was Alex Haley. He came up the stairs full of energy, carrying books under his arm. My sons and I were living on the top floor of a house. He sat on a gray silk couch and we talked about young marriages which we both had experienced. He told me that he was writing a book that would trace his ancestors back to West Africa. Although I had been to West Africa with my husband for six months and knew it had changed my entire consciousness, I still laughed. The idea of a person tracing his family back that far was funny to me. "You shouldn't laugh," he said very genially, "in fact you should trace yours." I never forgot it.

Joseph Papp

Before I left New York, Joe Papp, who has one of the most fluid minds of anyone I've met, had commissioned me to write a play for the Public Theatre. I was introduced to Joe by Ellen Holly who had been in many of his productions in Central Park and who had starred so exquisitely in *The Owl Answers* at the De Lys. It was because Joe had liked the production that he decided to commission me.

During that year we corresponded. I worked hard on a play called *Cities in Bezique* and sent it to Joe. He didn't say that he didn't like the play but after a time wrote back that he had decided to perform two other one-act plays of mine but could he use the title *Cities in Bezique* for them—which he did.

John Lennon and Paul McCartney

Pages of *The Lennon Play* were in Maschler's office. Everything was at a standstill. One of the people I was supposed to call in London was Nan Lanier. Billie Allen who had so movingly portrayed the tortured Sarah in *Funnyhouse* at the East

End Theatre had given me Nan's number, reminding me that she had helped form the American Place Theatre and was now living in London and like myself had small children. I called Nan.

"Our children can play in the garden," she said. Adam, Joey, and I walked to Hampstead on a lovely summer afternoon. When we arrived the very large house was filled with children running up and down stairs and several of Nan's friends. She asked what I was doing in London. I told her about *The Lennon Play*. "My best friend was in the Beatles movies," she said. It was Victor Spinetti and he was in *The Odd Couple* in the West End. Nan sent me to see him. "I'd love to direct it," he said. "I'll show the script to John." He took the script to John in Weybridge. Lennon promised to at least meet me.

It was at a studio somewhere off Picadilly Circus. *The Odd Couple,* which Spinetti starred in, was playing at a theatre nearby. The street entrance was small and dark and narrow steps led to a small room. Paul McCartney was there when we arrived. He was sitting on a long table. This room of the studio was small with a couple of desks cluttered with papers and one or two people busily phoning. McCartney was relaxed and friendly. "I Wanna Hold Your Hand" had been my six-year-old son Adam's favorite song. He stared up at the Beatle who laughed and playfully sat him on his knee. I had a postcard with me that I asked him to sign. He wrote, "To Adam, Paul McCartney." I placed it on the mantelpiece in our house where it was admired for almost a year. And then mysteriously the postcard was stolen.

We waited about twenty minutes and were about to leave and had come to the top of the stairs when Lennon came running up them. He wore a jean-type jacket and sneakers; he had disheveled hair and wore sunglasses. He fixed his eyes directly on us.

"This is John Lennon," Victor said.

"This is my son Adam," I said, *staring* at Lennon. He looked down at Adam.

"Hello, my son Adam," he said.

Inside the studio they were waiting for him. Victor said a few words and Lennon nodded good-bye and went in.

Fay Weldon

The Weldons lived on the end of Chalcot Crescent, three doors from Regent's Park Road. As I lived on the other end of Chalcot Crescent, very often I would walk past Fay Weldon's house. The English novelist (who is also credited with writing the first episode of Masterpiece Theatre) wrote at a desk by the window that faced the street. "If I look up and wave, that means please stop and come in for a cup of tea," she said. A very lively person, she always had wry stories to tell about her children, her husband, and their house. As I passed the house one morning she waved. Nonetheless, as I came up the path and she stood at the door she did not have her usual smile. There were tears in her eyes. She asked had I heard of a most famous English poet. I said yes. She said her close friend had lived in the country with him and had loved him very much but she was so deeply unhappy that on that very morning she had killed herself.

Victor Spinetti

I was one of the guests that Victor Spinetti invited to visit his family in Wales for the weekend. He led us on a long walk

111

through the heather up behind his house. The town looked just like *How Green Was My Valley*.

Michael Weller

When I had been in London for a few days, the very first person I got a letter from was Mike Weller. I had never met him but we both had had plays produced in Rome at the same theatre. Mike was still in Rome but said he would soon be in London to live and hoped we could meet. After we met he would sometimes stop in at Chalcot Crescent where I lived. One afternoon he suggested we have lunch in Chelsea. Mike was in his early twenties, an intense young writer with deep feelings about the world and its shortcomings. Inevitably, at lunch we began to discuss the United States, our lives in London, and racial problems.

"What I always felt," I said, "is that I don't belong."

The young writer looked at me and said, "but is it worth belonging to?"

John Lennon

The next time I saw him was at lunch next door at the National Theatre. I remember nothing of it except Victor Spinetti, Ringo Starr, John Lennon, George Martin, and I sat at a table while all the cast of the Young Vic looked on.

A Guest at a House in Maida Vale

He was a viscount and had known Churchill. We talked about the Brontës. I had not yet been to Haworth. In Primrose Hill, late at night, when I was lonely, I read British history.

My mother came to England for a visit. Now divorced from my father, she no longer said in passionate sentences,

"C. W., C. W.," my father's name. I remembered how she had cried at *Carrie*. "His eyes," she said, "I like Olivier's eyes."

Laurence Olivier (1967)

I met Olivier. He came across the rehearsal hall at the Old Vic and sat next to me. We were introduced. The director said Olivier had been very sick. He was pale. That was the fall morning that Lennon came to rehearsal dressed in a navy overcoat. Olivier had a shy smile as he watched a brief re-hearsal that Tynan and the director dominated. When the re-hearsal was over I set out for Waterloo Station to get the Un-derground back to Primrose Hill but turned and ran back to the theatre. Olivier was in the foyer with Tynan. I asked Oliv-ier for his autograph. He signed it on a tiny piece of torn pa-per. It would be stolen along with Lennon's and McCartney's.

George Harrison and his wife, Patti Harrison

They came to a party near Baker Street given by Victor Spin-etti, who had starred with the Beatles in both *Hard Day's Night* and *Help,* for the cast of the Young Vic. The Young Vic was to do a single performance of *The Lennon Play.* George Harrison had on a pink suit and Patti had on a vivid green chiffon dress and matching green chiffon boots. Harrison was very quiet and stood in the foyer watching unless someone ap-proached him to talk. Patti Harrison was extremely vivacious and moved about laughing and talking to everyone.

James Baldwin

A young actress who had been in a play of mine told me that she had been spending a lot of time with Jimmy Baldwin and his brother David. Baldwin was living somewhere near

Chelsea and was feeling a little lonely and wouldn't it be a great idea if we gave a party for him. She mentioned it to Baldwin and he said he would be delighted. My good friends Ann and Carlton Colcord joined in. The party was to be at my house. We brought cases of wine, cases of liquor and made huge pans of spinach lasagna. A friend insisted upon bringing his entire light show. A young musician said he'd bring his band. We rented chairs and tables from Harrod's. People phoned and asked what to wear. We lit the house with candles. All came. Some even came early. The band came, the light show lit one whole room. People were excited. Then Baldwin came with his English publisher. He talked to people and people talked to him.

Laurence Olivier (1967)

The tryout performance of *The Lennon Play* was a Sunday night in December at the National Theatre. I was told by Laurence Olivier that I would be seated next to him. I had adapted the books for the stage along with actor Victor Spinetti. Now Olivier was to judge from this performance whether or not he wanted to go on with the project. We were having dinner in the pub next door to the National — Kenneth Tynan, John and Penelope Mortimer, Olivier, and myself. "Laurence Olivier," I said, "I can't believe it." Tynan said, "Would you please stop saying, Laurence Olivier, I can't believe it?" The Mortimers smiled. After dinner we went outside and up the steps to the National Theatre. A long line had formed waiting for the possibility of seeing John Lennon, who came to the performance with his wife, Cynthia Lennon. One of my best friends, an American named Ann Colcord, stood in front. "Hi, Ann," I said. Olivier was holding my arm.

We went inside and indeed the others scattered and Olivier and I were seated together in the first row of the orchestra.

Sean Connery and Robert Stephens walked by. Olivier insisted upon holding my hand throughout the play and even turned often to stare at me. I was in a state of amazement. Right after the play ended, he disappeared saying he had to go home. The next morning when I called the director of the play he said that Olivier had liked the play and definitely wanted to go on with the project that spring. Definitely. But most likely without me. "In fact, Larry made up his mind that he wanted John Lennon himself to adapt the work."

John Lennon (1967)

It was a Saturday afternoon three weeks after the Sunday performance of the play at the National Theatre. About six in the evening the phone rang. I went downstairs to answer it. "Adrienne," he said, "this is John. What's it all about?" Earlier that week an English poet and friend of mine suggested he get John Lennon's address. He knew one person who had it and thought that we should send Lennon a telegram. He thought Lennon should know that I was being asked out of the project. He was positive Lennon wasn't a part of it. Well, the telegram had arrived in Weybridge and Lennon was on the phone. "John," I said, "after working on this play for almost a year I hear they want me out of it. I can't reach anyone on the phone." Lennon was silent, then he said, "I'll tell you what, let's all meet at Apple on Monday afternoon and clear the air. We have to do it now because I'll be going to India soon. Too . . . loo," he said.

It was a dark winter afternoon. Apple was the Beatles' business offices near Grosvenor Square. I arrived at the same time the director of the play did. Inside the offices people were running hither and thither. Lennon was talking to a young man with curly hair, but as soon as he saw us he suggested we go into an office. The office was very small and bare. John sat behind the desk. In appearance he was far from the Beatle image: his skin was extraordinarily pale and his brown hair was disheveled. The then fashionable gray mod jacket seemed far too big. Yet he seemed to radiate energy. He seemed full of life.

"I've told Olivier and Tynan that we will phone them while we're all here and settle this." He picked up the phone and got Tynan immediately, then beckoned to me to come to the desk. "I don't want Adrienne Kennedy put out of the play," he told Tynan. "Now you talk to him," he said and handed the phone to me. On the other end of the phone Tynan stuttered something about a misunderstanding and we all would meet next week in his office. John looked at me. Gently he said, "It's all settled." He got up from the desk and went to the door, and opened it, leaving the director and myself behind. About to exit, he said "tooloo."

Paris, 1968
Jean Marie Serreau

I went to Paris to a rehearsal of *Funnyhouse of a Negro*. It was winter. The day before I left London I developed a terrible cold. The hotel was near the Odéon. I remember the room seemed a haze. The entire weekend I clutched a bottle of an unknown French cold medicine. From the moment I arrived in Paris I had become weak and had to immediately go to the drugstore near the Odéon for medicine suggested by the director, Jean Marie Serreau. So all weekend I clutched a bottle of medicine right inside my purse.

Upstairs over the Odéon in a very small studio Jean Marie Serreau had me read a monologue from *Funnyhouse*. "I want to hear your voice and how you emphasize the lines. I want to be sure we have the monologues as you meant them." I read from Sarah's third monologue (my favorite). "I always dreamed of a day when my mother smiled at me . . ."

The French actors enclosed me in a circle. After the rehearsal of *Funnyhouse,* Serreau said to me, "Is there anyone, anyone in Paris you would like to meet?" I was so excited I couldn't think of one person.

Jean Louis Barrault

The Petit Odéon was run by Jean Louis Barrault and his wife, Madeline Renaud. The director Serreau told me that Mr. Barrault would come to a rehearsal of my play that afternoon. I could not believe this. My head swam at the thought of meeting Barrault. Serreau then took me on a long, exciting tour of the Odéon, speaking partly in French, telling me of the famous theatre's history. At the end of the tour we started to descend a very long, winding marble staircase that led to a dimly lit foyer with marble columns. Just as we came down into the foyer, Serreau exclaimed, "Oh, Madame Kennedy, here he is now!" And directly in front of me stood Jean Louis Barrault.

"Enchanté," he said, "enchanté." And he kissed my hand.

They spoke a few words in rapid French and Barrault vanished. Serreau said that Barrault would join us in rehearsal in a few moments. In a daze I started to walk and bumped into a marble column.

At the rehearsal Barrault sat three seats from me. In high school my friends Barbara and Rachel had taken me to see a French movie, *Infants of Paradise*. Barbara and Rachel could wondrously translate the movie's French lines. Barrault is great they said as we walked up the aisle out into the lobby of the movie theatre. Now in Paris after the rehearsal and dinner at one of the actor's houses I went back to the bleak hotel room. There was something wonderful about being faint and feverish from French cold medicine a few steps away from the majestic Odéon. The last time I had been in Paris I had been with my husband, Joe. I bought a tortoise shell fan at a stall on the Seine.

London, 1968

I continued to work on my play *Cities in Bezique* for the Public Theatre, sitting at the round dark dining table in the green wallpapered room overlooking the Crescent. This play would be too chaotic and abstract for Joe Papp, but he would use the title for his huge production of two of my other one-act plays, *The Owl Answers* and *Beast Story*. I would fly to New York at Christmas for the opening night where my father would be waiting for me at the Holiday Inn on West 57th Street. My father had already made a small scrapbook of assorted publicity clippings from the daily papers: he was hardly recognizable, stooped, somber, but ecstatic over the pile of clippings. He read me one from the *Post*. His pretty second wife had been killed suddenly in an automobile accident on the road near their Georgia house. And he had never recovered from this.

But for now, in London, I continued to respond to Joe Papp's letters of inquiry asking me when I would have a draft and telling me he was producing a play called *Hair*.

I also continued my brief mystery stories. Bill Gaskill was the head of the Royal Court. He gave teas. I believe they were on Tuesday afternoons. People I saw at those teas were John Osborne, Lord Snowdon, Jane Asher, and Edward Bond. One of the best productions I ever saw there was *The Three Sisters* with Marianne Faithfull. I was intrigued by the red-carpeted lobby, the backstage passages, so I used the Court in one of my incomplete mystery stories. The hero was in a play called *Twins* at the Court: my heroine was in love with him (a popular British film star as famous as Michael Caine or Finney) and went to the theatre every night. One night he confides to her, "Sometimes I believe I may be in danger, danger I can't define. Tonight on stage I was so nervous I got stage blood from my hand all over my face." She says we talked no more of danger but I could not stop staring at the smeared traces of stage blood at the edge of his blond hairline. His jealous twin brother, an actor himself, was at that moment planning the hero's murder, after which the brother and the hero's wife would live concealed in Yorkshire near Wordsworth's house.

I never finished these partial stories. But by reading of the lives of Elizabeth I (by Elizabeth Jenkins) and Queen Victoria (by Elizabeth Longford) murder, ambition, greed, and political as well as personal power were kept fresh in my mind.

I continued writing in the dining room overlooking the Crescent.

In the last part of my mystery story S., still trying to solve the circumstances surrounding J.'s death in Italy, accidentally stumbles upon the murderer, J.'s twin brother, in Yorkshire where he has hidden. She ends up sobbing out on the moors because, although she visits him, she cannot get him to answer any of her questions. And has to be dragged sobbing back across the moors to the nearby cottage where she is staying with the British playwright, W., her only friend in England.

I also continued to write impressions of people I met.

Allen Ginsberg

He read at a poetry reading that included Stephen Spender. At the party afterward he kissed my hand.

Anjelica Huston

She wore a ring that Marlon Brando had given her when she was a little girl.

119

Terence Stamp

I danced with him on the opening night of *Hair* on the stage after the performance.

Michael Caine

He was at the opening night of *Hair* with Bianca (later to be Jagger). She had on a tall hat.

Michael X

In 1981 I read an essay by a famous writer defining Michael as a murderer. In Trinidad he had been accused of digging holes then throwing corpses of former associates into them after having them butchered. He was later hanged. It was the end of a long personal and political odyssey. Before he was hanged I had been part of a small fund-raising effort along with Trixie Bullins, wife of the famed playwright Ed Bullins, to help Michael with legal fees. The Lennons had supported Michael and their endorsements of him were on a huge yellow poster that hung in my kitchen in New York for more than a year. The fund-raising efforts failed. Before he was hanged I received a letter from him recalling the summer Sunday afternoon we had spent at English playwright John Arden's and his wife, Margaretta D'arcy's, house. The Ardens lived in North London in rundown charm with their beautiful children running up and down steps and disappearing into rooms of toys.

We sat in an upstairs parlor . . . a lovely English Sunday. Michael said he had seen me walking in Primrose Hill and knew I was in London on a Guggenheim and also that I was working on the adaptation of Lennon's books. He had a much publicized friendship with the Beatles. He seemed to know all about me. Everything he said was in a soft voice, and one of his children, a little girl, hung gently on his arm. He said he belonged to an organization that wanted to kill all the policemen in England. And talked about his political ideas and activities. We had tea, then Michael said he wanted to talk to me privately and asked the Ardens if we could walk downstairs to the room on the main level. The room had a mantle, drawings, and a few books in a glass case. Michael was very quiet, almost shy. He said, "I arranged this meeting today because there's something I want to ask you." "Yes," I said, not knowing what to expect from a man who wanted to kill all the policemen in England. "I want you to teach me to write plays," he said very quietly. "Would you please think about it? I would appreciate it very much if you would give me lessons. I want to learn to write plays." I said I would think about it. He smiled and walked over to a window and gazed out. We went upstairs and the Ardens drove us home and we stopped at Michael's house in Islington. His wife, a small beautiful West Indian woman, came to the door. Their children played in the yard.

In one of my stories I gave myself an estranged twin sister, an actress whom I saw on stage (not realizing she was my sister because of her elaborate disguise). My children and I were also continual characters in my stories. Unlike in my stories my son Joe was not always in London. He spent all of the school year with Joe in Sierra Leona but came on long summers and school holidays.

Joe Chaikin

I had met Joe Chaikin once or twice in the Village in New York but didn't really get to talk to him until he came to London and we were both dinner guests of English poet Adrian Mitchell and his wife Celia at their home in Hampstead. Joe and I agreed after dinner to meet again in a day or so. I invited him to come to Primrose Hill for a drink. He arrived on a beautiful summer afternoon. He either said he had been on a European tour of the Open Theatre or he was starting one. But at any rate, he had about one hour before he had to rush out to more rehearsals. I led him to the main room which overlooked a walled garden, overgrown, but nonetheless charming and tranquil. Joe sat down on the couch and said he'd really been working hard. We decided to have a cold drink. I went to the kitchen which was a flight of stairs down and got the drinks. When I came back up the stairs and into the room Joe had fallen sound asleep. I woke him in an hour so he could go to rehearsals.

David Mercer

During intermission at the Royal Court very often people would go to the pub next door. At one of these intermissions I found myself standing next to playwright David Mercer, best known at that time for his screenplay of *Morgan*. I had met David when I first came to London. He was a very direct person.

"Are you still here?" he asked. I had been in London for about fourteen months. I nodded, yes. "Why?" he asked. He then referred to the tumultuous racial and social scene in the U.S. and yet *here* I was.

"Isn't it a washout?" he asked.

His comment was a turning point in my life in London. When I recently read his obituary in *The New York Times*, I understood that I owed him something.

I worked on my play for the Public Theatre as I sat in the pale-green wallpapered dining room that faced Chalcot Crescent. The plot was not clear. An English history book I'd bought on Shaftesbury Ave. lay on the dark table. How drawn I was to its passages.

"In the palace guards have been doubled and pensioners armed. The Queen's jewelry and silver have been sent to be guarded with the crown jewels and many private persons conceal themselves. Many of the ministers are hated by the people. The minds of all are in great perturbation. There is great anxiety. Great storms have overturned steeples. Forests have been uprooted and thousand of trees have fallen. Racial wars abound."

1969

Often there seemed to be a mystery surrounding events: Sylvia Plath had lived in Chalcot Square. Karl Marx had walked in Primrose Hill. The mystery pervaded the English dusk of Chalcot Road as I walked to its end and Primrose Hill School with its black iron fence in late December afternoons to pick up Adam and take him to tea. One family we visited often had children whose names were Sebastian and Albertine. They had a pet monkey and a small drawing room lined with dozens of narrow shelves of miniature toys. On some nights I wrote mystery stories inspired by famous British murders and made myself and the children characters. One included a description of our real house.

"Chalcot Crescent was beautiful: We lived on two floors of the house at Number 37. It was furnished and belonged to an English family that was in Nigeria. The faded parlor faced a wild garden with a brick wall. The boys had a large sunny room on the lower level. My room, the master bedroom, was the prettiest, shuttered and decorated in dark rose. All the houses on the curved crescent were painted white. Our door was a lovely yellow. The children were thrilled because the television series 'The Avengers' was filmed on the Crescent. The exterior of the corner house was used for 'The Avengers' to emerge from and pursue their enemies. We loved our house but were afraid of the spiders in the bathroom that came up the drain from the garden."

Soon there would be rallies in Trafalgar Square against the war in Vietnam. More that once Vanessa Redgrave led them.

The crazed old woman living in the house on Rothwell Street screamed, standing in the yard, some days, "Go back to India where you belong." Despite the enchantment, there was a subplot to England that I couldn't perceive. And although I could never admit it, the hurt over the breakup of my marriage had never healed. I thought: Perhaps I should go home. And I did.

Adrienne Kennedy began to write and have her plays produced in the 1960s. She has been commissioned to write plays for the Public Theater, Jerome Robbins, The Royal Court, the Mark Taper Forum, and Juilliard. Kennedy has been a visiting lecturer at many universities, including Yale, Princeton, Brown, and the University of California, Berkeley, and currently is a visiting professor at Stanford. She will teach at Harvard University in 1990. Kennedy's plays have been part of college curricula in the United States, Europe, and Africa. Her 1964 Obie Award-winning play, *Funnyhouse of a Negro,* was broadcast by the BBC and Radio Denmark, and has been translated into several languages. Kennedy is one of five playwrights included in the *Norton Anthology of American Literature*, third edition, volume 2. Kennedy's most recent play is *She Talks to Beethoven. Adrienne Kennedy in One Act* was published by Minnesota in 1988, and her autobiography, *People Who Led to My Plays,* was published by Knopf in 1987. She received the Third Annual Manhattan Borough President's Award for Excellence in the Arts for 1988.